7 Simple Steps to Unclutter Your Life

7 Simple Steps to Unclutter Your Life

Donna Smallin

STOREY
BOOKS

Schoolhouse Road
Pownal, Vermont 05261

The mission of Storey Communications is to serve our customers by publishing practical information that encourages personal independence in harmony with the environment.

Edited by Deborah Balmuth and Robin Catalano
Cover design by Meredith Maker
Cover and interior illustrations by Carleen Powell
Text design by Susan Bernier
Text production by Jennifer Jepson Smith
Indexed by Peggy Holloway, Holloway Indexing Services

The information in this book is true and complete to the best of our knowledge. All recommendations are made without guarantee on the part of the author or Storey Books. The author and publisher disclaim any liability in connection with the use of this information. For additional information, please contact Storey Books, Schoolhouse Road, Pownal, Vermont 05261.

Storey books are available for special premium and promotional uses and for customized editions. For further information, please call Storey's Custom Publishing Department at 1-800-793-9396.

Printed in the United States by R. R. Donnelley
10 9 8 7 6 5 4 3 2

Library of Congress Cataloging-in-Publication Data

Smallin, Donna, 1960–
    7 simple steps to unclutter your life / Donna Smallin.
        p.   cm.
    ISBN 1-58017-237-7 (pbk. : alk. paper)
    1. Home economics. 2. Time management. I Title: Seven simple steps to unclutter your life. II. Title.
  TX147.S62   2000
  640—dc21   99-053488

Contents

Dedication

For Mom and Dad,
who turned out all right after all.

Acknowledgments

Many thanks to my research assistant, Monica Schurr, who unearthed excellent reference materials, tracked down obscure details, and generously contributed her own ideas. I also want to thank my husband and family (especially you, Gramma), for inspiring and encouraging me to live a simpler life. Special thanks go to my publisher for giving me this opportunity to share what I have learned, and to Robin Catalano, my editor, for pulling it together so beautifully.

Introduction

There have been many times in my life when I wanted to scream, "Stop the world — I want to get off!" What I really wanted was to stop time, so that I could catch up on everything that had to be done.

I used to make long lists of things to do and, like everyone who writes lists, I enjoyed the satisfaction of crossing off each task as I completed it. But the list was endless. There was always too much to do and too little time in which to do it.

Not only did I not have enough time, I never had enough money. I earned a decent income, but the money went out as quickly as it came in — sometimes faster. I felt like I was working for nothing.

Then I took a five-day bicycle trip that changed my life. It was my first vacation in four years. I rode 40 to 70 miles each day and camped out with about 400 other cyclists. Occasionally other cyclists accompanied me, but mostly I rode alone. So I had plenty of time to think.

One day, it dawned on me what was wrong with my life. I had been "pedaling along" not even realizing that I was lost. I was not living true to myself or my values. I wasn't even sure who I was anymore. All I knew for sure was that I was unhappy.

I was unhappy because I had made some bad choices — about how I spent my time, money, and energy — and I was living with the consequences of those choices. Thankfully, I realized that I didn't have to live with those consequences forever. With the support of friends and family, I found the courage to make new choices.

I share this with you to make an important point. If there's something that's not working in your life, only you can make it right. That's what this book is all about: making your life right again. *Because you deserve to be happy.*

> *The grand essentials of happiness are something to do, something to love, and something to hope for.*
>
> — Allan K. Chalmers

Simplicity in Seven Steps

Something made you pick up this book. Does it feel as if your life is spinning out of control? Are you feeling stressed out? Lost? Unhappy? Do you wish you had more time to spend with family and friends? More time to enjoy life? Less debt? More savings? Or are you feeling so confused and helpless that you don't know who you are or what you want?

What you'll find in this book are seven simple steps plus hundreds of practical tips and ideas for uncluttering and improving the quality of your life. I promise you this: If you put even a fraction of these tips into practice, you will begin to create a simpler, happier, more satisfying life *immediately*.

Put Yourself First

In this chapter . . .

- *Regain Control*
- *Boost Your Energy*
- *Maintain a Healthy Weight*
- *Get Fit for Life*
- *Practice Wellness*
- *Drink to Your Health*
- *Pamper Yourself*

I t's not easy juggling multiple priorities, especially when it means juggling the demands of family and career along with your own needs. And yet that's what we do day after day after day. Some days we accomplish extraordinary things and even manage to keep everyone happy. But at what cost?

No matter how valiantly we try, we can't do everything all of the time. And we can't do some things as often or as well as we would like to do them. So we wind up feeling like we've failed somehow. We're stressed out, tired, and maybe even a little angry. More often than not, we sacrifice our own plans and goals to meet the needs of others. Or we don't even *make* plans and goals for ourselves because we figure, "Why bother?"

Yes, family is important. Yes, work is important. And yes, there's only so much time in a day. But if you don't take care of your own needs, who will?

If you want to unclutter your life, begin by choosing to put yourself first. It's not being selfish; it's being self-caring. There's a big difference. Caring for yourself — physically, emotionally, intellectually, socially, and spiritually — will make you happier, healthier, and better able to cope with the demands of daily living. In fact, by putting your own needs first and reserving even just a little more time and energy for yourself, you will have more to give to others.

Regain Control

Wouldn't it be wonderful if we could stop time long enough to get caught up? Well, maybe someday time travel will become a reality and we can do just that. Meanwhile, time keeps on ticking. But time is not the enemy. It's how we choose to spend our precious time that determines how fulfilling our lives are.

Somewhere along the way, we got into the habit of going, going, going all the time. We've been doing it for so long, we rarely stop to think about what we're doing and if it really matters. We just get up each morning, get on the treadmill of life, and go. Why? Because we have to keep up with the rest of the world. Says who?

A Matter of Perspective

As long as everyone around us is racing through life at warp speed, we feel compelled to keep up. But one thing we tend to forget, especially when the pace gets hectic, is that we do have a say in how we live our lives. And if the pace is getting too intense, we can choose to slow down — a little or a lot.

Perception is reality. If you're feeling like you're overwhelmed, you *are* overwhelmed. But you can regain some control over your life. And now is just as good a time as any.

It's okay to hop off the treadmill, or just slow the pace. Life will go on, perhaps more leisurely. That wouldn't be so bad, would it?

Before you go to bed tonight, start a list of things you've been putting off — things you would like to do if only you had the time. In the morning when you get dressed, make a point to wear something you love, like a favorite sweater, scarf, or piece of jewelry. Throughout the day, every time you catch a glimpse of yourself in a mirror, think of one thing you would really love to do and say to yourself, "I make time for other things. I can make time for this too."

Take action. Do one special thing for yourself today. Buy yourself a bouquet of flowers, paint your toenails, or simply go outside tonight and wish upon a star.

Ask for help. So often, we want and need help but don't ask. Asking for help is not a sign of weakness; it takes courage to ask for help. Once you admit to needing help, you may find that it comes from the most unexpected sources.

Document your day. In your diary or on a sheet of notebook paper, jot down everything you do from the time you wake up until the time you go to bed. Try to account for every hour. Do this every day for a full week. At the end of the week, take a look at how you spent your time. Then determine where you can cut back to free up some "you" time.

Make an appointment with yourself. Schedule *your* time into your daily planner and keep your appointment.

Making It Work

Commit to putting yourself first for three weeks. Try not to let anyone or anything interfere with *your* time. Really give it your best effort. If you're concerned about taking time away from other people and things, remind yourself that it's only for three weeks. At the end of that time, ask yourself what, if anything, you lost and what you gained. In all likelihood, the gain will outweigh the loss. *Bonus:* Because it takes 21 days to establish new habits, after three weeks your new routine will be easier to maintain.

Keep a journal. Jot down what you've done for yourself each day. How did it make you feel? How did your family, friends, boss, and colleagues react? If you weren't able to keep your appointment with yourself, describe why. What happened? How can you prevent it from interfering with your time in the future?

Start small. Start by giving yourself the gift of 15 minutes each day to do something you really enjoy or have been wanting to do. Get up 15 minutes earlier if you have to, but try to carve it out of your existing day if you can. You can do quite a lot in 15 minutes when you focus your energies. But keep in mind that this is not the time to clean the house or get the kids' lunches ready for school; it's your time to do something for you.

Create a positive self-image. Act as if you are a person with an extraordinary ability to nurture and care for yourself and you will become that person.

Boost Your Energy

Whether you're a couch potato or an athlete, your body needs fuel to function. The more efficient the fuel, the more energy it provides. If you feel like taking a nap after lunch or you tend to crave sweets and carbohydrates, your body is trying to tell you something: The fuel you're giving it is insufficient for the demands of daily living.

To fuel your body efficiently, you'll want to eat a well-balanced diet. If your eyes are already starting to glaze over at the thought of having to figure out the proper ratio of proteins, carbohydrates, and fats (not to mention vitamins and minerals), relax. You don't have to understand all the ins and outs of proper nutrition to eat well.

Nourish Yourself

While each person's nutritional needs vary, following these simple guidelines will get you in the ballpark of good nutrition:

- Eat foods in their natural state as often as possible: for example, raw fruits and vegetables, beans, nuts, and seeds.
- Choose whole grains (whole wheat, oat, bran) over more refined and processed grains in pasta, breads, and cereals.
- Eat two fruits or vegetables at each meal.
- Eat no more than one or two servings daily of fish, chicken, turkey, lean beef, or pork. A serving is about 3 ounces, or the size of a deck of cards. If you are a vegetarian, be sure to get an adequate amount of protein, preferably from legumes.
- Choose skim or 1% milk over whole milk, and nonfat or low-fat cheeses over regular cheeses.
- Eat fruit, bagels, or English muffins instead of doughnuts, cakes, cookies, and pastries.
- Go light on butter, margarine, and oils as well as sugar, salt, and alcohol.

- Eat a variety of foods.
- Drink at least eight 8-ounce glasses of water each day — more on days you exercise.

Don't eat too much. Eat three meals a day, but stick with one regular-size helping at each meal. You can eat a light snack between meals if you get hungry. (See ideas for nutritious snacks on page 10.)

Don't eat too little. Calories equal energy. You need a certain number of calories just to get you through your day. Even if you're trying to lose weight, you should still eat three meals a day. Consuming too few calories can cause your body to enter a protective state in which your metabolism slows down and begins to store fat because it thinks you're starving!

Don't skip breakfast. Eating a healthy breakfast provides fuel for your mind and body. Here are some ideas for energy-boosting breakfasts:

- Nonfat or low-fat yogurt and an English muffin spread lightly with jam
- Cereal with nonfat or 1% milk and sliced fruit, plus a slice of whole wheat toast spread very lightly with peanut butter
- Nonfat or low-fat cottage cheese with sliced peaches and whole wheat toast spread lightly with jam
- Hot oatmeal with raisins and skim milk

- A toasted English muffin topped with one slice of lean ham or turkey and/or low-fat cheese and then broiled, plus a piece of fruit
- Scrambled eggs (one or two) sprinkled with shredded low-fat cheese and rolled up in a whole wheat tortilla with salsa on top

HEALTHY SHOPPING

When shopping for groceries, spend more time around the perimeter of the store, where you'll find fruits and vegetables, breads, fish, meats, and dairy products. With the exception of cereals, grains, pastas, herbs, and some frozen foods, the inner aisles in a grocery store contain mostly processed or junk foods. Shop with a list and buy only what's on your list. Shop as quickly as you can; it's been proved that the more time you spend in the store, the more you will spend (and it's usually on junk food).

Nutritious Snacks

When you're hungry, you'll eat anything, so plan to have a healthy snack between breakfast and lunch and again between lunch and dinner. Following are some healthy, tasty, and satisfying between-meal snacks:

- Cherry tomatoes
- Carrot sticks with hummus
- Precut vegetables with nonfat sour cream dip

- Frozen grapes or banana slices
- Pumpkin seeds
- Dates or raisins
- English muffin with low-sugar jam
- Low-fat cereal bar
- Crunchy snacks such as pretzels, breadsticks, and air-popped popcorn
- Skim milk with low-calorie chocolate syrup or a mug of nonfat hot chocolate

Maintain a Healthy Weight

One of the best ways to take care of yourself is to maintain a healthy weight, which for many of us means shedding a few pounds. And there's only one way to do it: For every pound you want to lose, you've got to "lose" 3,600 calories. You do that by either consuming 3,600 fewer calories or burning them off through exercise. It's simple — in theory, anyway.

In practice, reaching and maintaining a healthy weight can be a lifelong battle. But it's a battle that's well worth the fight, especially if you spend a lot of time or energy worrying about your weight, or if you don't feel good about yourself because of your weight.

Maintaining a healthy weight will not only boost your energy, but also can reduce your risk of heart disease, diabetes, cancer, and a variety of other medical problems that can complicate your life. It's the single best thing you can do for yourself.

Take it off! If you are more than 10 percent over your healthy weight, aim for one to two pounds of weight loss per week.

Remember: To lose weight, you need to consume fewer calories, burn more, or both. If you walk at a moderate pace for 30 minutes every day, eat sensibly, and cut out a couple of desserts a week, you could lose about one pound in a week.

Avoid fad diets, especially diets that severely restrict caloric intake or entire groups of foods. You may lose weight quickly following one fad or another, but quick weight loss is usually followed by quick weight gain.

Be patient. Allow yourself time to achieve your healthy weight. Once you get going, weight loss adds up fast. Do the math: A loss of 1 pound a week adds up to 52 pounds in a year!

Make small changes. If you simply replace one 8-ounce glass of regular soda a day (100 calories) with water, you can lose 10 pounds in a year — painlessly.

True or false? Fat-free foods are guilt-free, so you can eat as much as you want. Sadly, this is false. Even nonfat foods can be fattening if you eat too much.

Control Is the Key

Live for today. In *Get Real: A Personal Guide to Real-Life Weight Management,* author Daniel Kosich, Ph.D., suggests that you focus on taking care of yourself today, not achieving some future weight goal. He also recommends applying the 80/20 rule to what you eat: Eat what you know you should 80 percent of the time and leave 20 percent for acknowledging and accepting that you're not perfect.

Remember that all foods are okay to eat — just not okay to eat at all times. So when you are tempted to eat a slice of gooey chocolate cake or buy a big bag of greasy potato chips, try saying to yourself, "I'm not going to eat this today because right now I'm trying to eat healthier foods. I can have that some other time." Recognizing that these foods are not forbidden forever makes it easier to turn them down.

Eat more earlier in the day and less later. If you can, make breakfast your biggest meal, followed by a substantial lunch and a very light supper. When you've finished what's on your plate, stop eating. If you still feel hungry, wait 20 minutes. It takes that long for your brain to register that your stomach is full.

Get a handle on portions. If you think you're eating the right stuff but still can't shake excess weight, reduce your portions. Americans tend to underestimate what they eat by 50 percent because they misunderstand serving sizes. For example, the bagel you eat for breakfast is most likely not one but two or even three servings of grains. The official USDA serving size for a bagel is 2 ounces — a far cry from the 4 to 6 ounces of the average bagel.

Dine out less often. It's easy to be tempted into eating high-fat, high-calorie foods when you order off a menu. Eating at home lets you maintain more control of what goes in your mouth (and onto your hips, thighs, or waist!).

If you're watching calories, watch what you drink. A glass of juice is a healthier choice than a glass of soda, but it has about the same amount of calories. Water is always the best choice. Coffee has zero calories, but the calories in sugar and creamer add up fast. Try nonfat creamer (liquid or powder).

Eat Out — Don't Pig Out

If you eat out often, you may want to try these fat- and calorie-busting ideas:

- Order a cup of soup (not cream-based) or a salad to help fill you up.
- Order salad dressing and sauces on the side. Dip the tines of your fork into the dressing or sauce and then into your food.
- Skip the appetizers, or split one with everyone at your table.
- Choose "heart-healthy" choices as indicated on the menu. Alternatively, choose entrées that are prepared simply: baked, broiled, or grilled fish, chicken, or steak.
- Before you dig into your meal, determine how much you will eat. Restaurant entrées are often the equivalent of two to three servings. Portion off the amount you plan to eat and stop eating when you have consumed that much. Take home leftovers only if they will not add excessive fat and calories to your diet the next day.
- Avoid cream sauces and anything fried, batter-dipped, or stuffed.
- Order a fruit juice spritzer, glass of tomato juice, or water.
- Skip dessert and have a decaffeinated cappuccino or herbal tea instead.
- If you dine out only occasionally, eat whatever you want and enjoy it. Just eat a little lighter the day before and the day after.

Reshape your attitude. Don't let being self-conscious about your body get in the way of participating in activities you enjoy, such as swimming, dancing, and cycling. You have the right to enjoy any activities regardless of your body shape or size. Remember that your self-esteem and identity come from within.

Cook lighter. Many recipes call for more sugar, salt, or fat than is really necessary. Try using half the amount of sugar and salt. Use two egg whites instead of a whole egg. Use nonstick pans or spray regular pans with nonstick cooking spray. Use half the amount of applesauce in place of oil, butter, or margarine in baked goods. You can also try fruit-based fat replacers, which are sold in most supermarkets.

Put success into perspective. Do honor your goal to be fit and healthy, but don't fret if you never lose that last 10 pounds or develop "killer abs." You are still a beautiful person with the potential to achieve a happy, healthy, successful life.

Eat less for dinner. This is one way to shave off a few hundred calories each day. The key is to decrease your appetite. Try eating a healthy midafternoon snack. Exercise for 30 to 60 minutes just prior to your evening meal. Drink a large glass of water before sitting down to eat, or eat a salad before your main course.

Read labels. You don't have to read everything on the label, but do look at serving size, fat, and calories. A 1999 survey by the American Dietetic Association shows that consumers who read food labels get 30 percent of their calories from fat; nonreaders get 35 percent. Look for products that have a big difference between the total calories and the number of fat calories.

Stop sampling. Reduce fat and calories by cutting back on sampling when you cook or bake.

Thinner isn't always better. If you eat right and exercise but can't seem to reach your ideal body weight, don't panic. First, consult with your physician to make sure there aren't any underlying problems. If everything checks out okay, relax. It's probable that your "ideal" is based on the media's idealistic — often unrealistic — body image.

Get Fit for Life

According to the Surgeon General's 1996 Report on Physical Activity and Health, more than 60 percent of adults do not engage in the recommended amount of physical activity — and 25 percent are not active at all. Yet a single workout can boost your energy, lift your spirits, and make you feel great.

In addition to helping to control weight, regular exercise over time can combat anxiety and depression, improve self-esteem, and help you better manage stress. It also can reduce your risk of heart disease, diabetes, and cancer.

Where Do I Begin?

Get physical. Engage in 30 minutes of moderate exercise every day. A moderate-intensity workout is the equivalent of a brisk 1½-mile walk in 30 minutes.

Start slow and easy. If you are just starting an exercise program, begin with 10 to 15 minutes a day at a pace that's comfortable for you. Over a period of a few weeks, gradually increase the length of your workout to 30 minutes or more each day. Then work on increasing your pace so that you can hear yourself breathing and feel your pulse quicken.

Choose an exercise you enjoy — and one that you can work into your schedule. Walking is ideal because it can be done anywhere by just about anyone. All you need is a sturdy, comfortable pair of walking shoes.

Stick with it. Get out and exercise even when you don't feel like going. Notice how you are feeling at the halfway point. More than likely, you'll be glad you made the extra effort to get out.

Break it up. To improve fitness, you'll want to strive for 30 minutes of exercise three to five times a week, but it doesn't have to be 30 consecutive minutes. Any physical activity that gets your heart beating faster counts. Here are some ways to fit a workout into your day:

- Walk or bike to the store (or to work) instead of driving.
- Get off your commuter bus or train one stop early and walk to work.
- Park your car on the perimeter of parking lots and walk.
- Walk on your lunch hour.
- Climb stairs instead of using the elevator.
- Put on music and dance while you're cleaning the house.
- Work out anger or frustration in your garden with a hoe.
- Rake leaves or sweep the sidewalk or driveway.
- Substitute 30 minutes of walking for watching a half-hour television program.
- Play active games with your kids.

Try circuit training. Circuit training combines strength training with aerobic exercise for a good all-around workout in a minimum amount of time. Using weights (either free weights or weight machines), you alternate exercises for the upper and lower body. This increases strength. If done quickly with minimal rest between exercises, it also increases cardiovascular endurance.

Rediscover the joy of playing! If the word *workout* keeps you from exercising, think of it as playtime. Try doing some of the things you used to do as a kid. Remember how much fun you had? Go for a bike ride. Walk to a friend's house. Swim at the community center pool. Or take a hike in the woods and pretend it's an adventure!

Just Move!

The American Heart Association has a health and fitness Web site that lets you keep track of your progress on-line and sign up for your very own personal trainer. Check it out at www.justmove.org. You also can ask for help or exchange stories with others who are participating in your choice of exercise. Click on "Cyber Teams" for more information.

Getting the Most out of Your Fitness Regimen

Take ten. When you and your kids enjoy a special treat like ice cream, follow it up with a 10-minute walk. It's a great way to spend quality time with your kids. You also can use this time to explore what's happening in your neighborhood.

Set goals. Even a small goal will get you out on days when you're just not in the mood to exercise. If walking or running is your exercise, pick a local race and train for it.

Exercise for a cause. There are lots of events that rely on walkers, runners, and cyclists to raise money for a cause. An event like this is a great motivator to get you into the swing.

Realize that doing something is better than doing nothing. If on some days you're feeling crunched for time or you're just not motivated to exercise, tell yourself that you're just going to do half today. You may find that once you get going, you'll want to keep going for your full routine. Even if you don't, you're still getting in some exercise, and some exercise is better than none!

Pump it up. If walking is your exercise of choice, pump your arms as you walk to increase the intensity of your workout. You can burn even more calories in a shorter time by walking hills. Warm up for 10 minutes first and then walk up at a steady, comfortable pace. Shorten your stride on the way down to protect your lower back and knees. Better yet, find a flatter route back.

Say, "Let's dance!" Dancing is a great way to get in a workout and have fun too. Maybe you can interest your partner in dance lessons — or have a little fun with your kids. Put on some music and try to dance through three to five songs (about 10 to 15 minutes). Let them choose the music one day and you can pick out the songs or choose the radio station the next day.

Involve your kids. Most kids need more exercise than they're getting. In fact, nearly two thirds of all school-age children can't measure up to the minimum standard of fitness. Find ways you can exercise together as a family such as walking, cycling, and in-line skating.

Combine exercise and social time. Make plans to walk, jog, cycle, dance, swim, or skate with a friend or group. Not only will you enjoy it more, but you'll be more motivated to keep it up as well.

Exercise early in the day. There are three benefits to exercising first thing in the morning:

1. It raises your metabolism, so you burn more calories all day long.
2. You may find you sleep better.
3. Most importantly, by putting your exercise first, you'll be more likely to do it every day.

Practice Wellness

Taking the time to eat well and exercise is the single best way to get — and stay — healthy. And being healthy makes you feel good about yourself, which makes you feel better about everything and everyone around you. In fact, developing a healthy lifestyle can give you a whole new perspective on life. You may find that the things that used to stress you out don't seem so stressful anymore.

Cultivate Good Habits

Treat your body with respect. Give it enough rest. Fuel it with a variety of foods. Exercise it appropriately, and listen to what it needs.

Call it quits. Smoking adds wrinkles around your eyes and mouth, stains your teeth, and makes your clothes and everything in your house dirty. It also increases your risk of heart attack, stroke, and lung and throat cancer. When you quit smoking, these risks eventually return to almost that of a nonsmoker. Don't wait until it's too late; do what you have to do now to quit. If you're afraid that you will gain weight, substitute daily exercise for smoking.

Find a doctor who is a good listener. You will be more apt to share your concerns and thereby alleviate unnecessary fears.

Make health and safety a priority. Always wear your seatbelt; it can save your life. If you ride a bicycle, wear a helmet. Head injuries are reported in 75 percent of all accidents involving bicycles. According to the Brain Injury Association of New York, helmets can decrease the risk of brain injury by 88 percent.

Celebrate wellness! Let your birthday be a reminder each year to schedule an annual physical exam. Regular checkups can help to catch potential health problems before they become serious. Taking better care of yourself now will help you live longer, with fewer disabilities and health problems.

See your dental hygienist twice a year. Don't have dental insurance? Have your teeth cleaned twice a year anyway. Regular cleanings prevent the buildup of plaque and tartar that can lead to tooth decay and more serious (and expensive) problems. The $60 to $70 you pay for each visit can save you hundreds and thousands of dollars in the long run and help you keep your teeth well into your senior years.

Floss! According to the January 1999 *Journal of Periodontology,* nearly one third of all Americans between the ages of 30 and 54 have periodontitis, an advanced stage of bone loss that has been linked to diabetes, respiratory disease, and heart attacks. The best prevention? Brush your teeth and remember to floss daily.

Wash your hands frequently. Soap and water are the best prevention against germs that can cause colds. Forget the antibacterial soap; any soap will do. For best results, wash your hands like nurses do: for a full 60 seconds. (To keep the tops of your hands from drying out, wash only the palms. Follow up with moisturizer.)

Get moving. The simplest prescription for many minor (and some major) illnesses is regular, moderate exercise. Whether you suffer from depression or varicose veins, high blood pressure or high cholesterol, hemorrhoids or menopausal hot flashes, a 30-minute walk four or five times a week can work wonders.

Drink to Your Health

Sufficient water consumption helps all of your vital organs (including your brain) function better. Lack of fluid intake can result in fatigue, weakness, listlessness, sore muscles, jitters, and even the blues. A good rule is to drink twice as much water as it takes to quench your thirst.

Water keeps your skin smooth and healthy. It helps minimize cellulite and wrinkles. And it can help to prevent common illnesses and medical problems such as constipation, hemorrhoids, headaches, urinary tract infections, colds, and flu. Drinking water flushes toxins out of the body. It also can help you lose weight because you feel more full.

Boost Your Water Intake

All liquids you drink count toward your daily intake, but water is the only drink that has curative as well as protective effects on our health. Drinking at least five glasses of water a day has been associated with a decreased risk of heart disease, stroke, and diabetes in men and women, as well as a decreased risk of bladder cancer in men.

Following are some tips for drinking more water, especially if you aren't currently drinking the recommended eight 8-ounce glasses daily:

- Drink a glass of water while you're waiting for your coffee to perk.
- Fill a sports bottle with water and ice and take it with you when you leave the house.
- Drink at least three glasses of water before lunchtime.
- Never pass a water fountain without stopping to drink from it.
- Drink a glass of water before — and during — every meal.
- Keep a pitcher of water in the refrigerator at all times.

If you hate the taste of plain water . . .

- Add a squeeze of fresh lemon, lime, or orange.
- Add a splash of cranberry juice.
- Put several slices of lemon into a pitcher of water to give it an ever-so-slight citrusy taste.
- Eat more juicy fruits and vegetables such as watermelons, cantaloupes, lettuce, cucumbers, and tomatoes.

- Drink plain seltzer water or seltzer diluted with up to 25 percent juice.
- Drink tea — hot or iced. Green tea and echinacea tea offer the added potential benefits of boosting your immune system.
- Replace some (not all) water with soft drinks, lemonade, low-fat or nonfat milk, juice, or broth soups.

Pamper Yourself

Isn't it time you did something nice for yourself? You don't have to spend a fortune and you don't have to wait for someone else to pamper you. Make it a point to pamper yourself regularly and whenever you're feeling down or want a quick pick-me-up.

Incorporate mini pampering sessions into your regular routine. When you apply hand and body cream, don't just rub it in; massage it in. For a rosy glow, use a daily facial scrub to exfoliate your skin. Find a shower gel with a fragrance you really enjoy and apply it with a loofah mitt or nylon sponge. Trade foot massages or back rubs with your partner.

Go to a spa-a-a-h. Treat yourself to a full-body massage, facial, pedicure, or manicure. Leave your worries at the door and enjoy a little bit of heaven on earth.

Wash away tension. If you've had a bad day, come home and take a shower and wash your worries away. Or relax in a hot tub with scented oil or bath salts.

Give yourself a pedicure. Soak your feet for 10 to 15 minutes in a dishpan filled with warm water and bubble bath, or take a bath. Dry feet thoroughly. Use a pumice stone to remove calluses. Trim toenails straight across and gently push back cuticles with a cuticle stick. To refresh feet, massage in peppermint foot cream. Apply nail polish for a finishing touch.

Send your laundry out. You may not want to do this every week, but if you are having a particularly hectic week, why not?

PLAN A ROMANTIC EVENING

A quality-time session with your significant other should be more than a once-in-a-while occasion. Invest some time and energy in preparing for a romantic interlude with your partner. Make a reservation at your favorite restaurant or plan a romantic dinner at home with candlelight and music. Think of ways you can make it an evening to remember. Planning is half the fun!

Buy sexy lingerie. No one sees what you're wearing under your business suit or casual attire, but if it's something sexy, it makes you feel sexy, and that's a treat in itself!

Order dinner and a movie. Pick up a video and something to eat on your way home or have dinner delivered and order a pay-per-view movie. Put your feet up and relax.

Cook yourself a gourmet meal. This is a wonderful way to treat yourself if you live alone. By taking the time to prepare yourself a nice meal, you are saying, "I'm worth it." And you know what? You *are* worth it!

Indulge your craving for chocolate. Don't worry; a little bit of chocolate once in a while is not going to kill you. In fact, chocolate contains antioxidants similar to those in red wine, so it may help you live longer!

Splurge on a fantasy. Do something you've always wanted to do.

Listen to music. Turn off the television and enjoy whatever is music to your ears. Put on your favorite CD or go outside and listen to the sounds of nature.

Plan a friends night out. Call your good friends and plan a night out with no kids and no spouses.

Get away. Pack a bag and retreat to your favorite destination. Or go visit a friend or family member whose company you really enjoy.

Pack a picnic. Or just get a sandwich and beverage from your favorite deli and head somewhere where you can relax with your thoughts.

Do nothing at all. Simply sit and enjoy a few moments of stillness.

Take a wellness day. Using a paid personal day or an unpaid day off, tell your boss you don't need a sick day but you do need a wellness day to help prevent you from getting sick! Then do whatever your heart desires on that day.

Have some scents. Place a jar of potpourri in your bedroom. Put scented sachets in your dresser drawers. Light fragranced candles. Match your perfume or cologne to to your mood each day.

Use flower power to brighten your day. Have flowers delivered to your home or stop at your local florist and buy yourself a big bouquet.

Live Authentically

In this chapter . . .

- *Question Everything*
- *Evaluate Your Values and Beliefs*
- *Commit to Change*
- *Create a New Vision*
- *Finding Your Balance*

L iving authentically requires an understanding of who you are and what's really important to you so that all decisions flow naturally and comfortably from within rather than without. It's about being true to yourself.

People who find themselves face to face with death learn quickly what's important to them. But you don't have to wait for a crisis to figure out what really matters. Do it now.

When you make a choice to live your life according to your values, you will find more time, less stress, and a sense of personal freedom. And isn't that what uncluttering your life is all about?

> *Why should the lord of the country*
> *Flit about like a fool?*
> *If you let yourself be blown to and fro,*
> *You lose touch with your root.*
> *If you let restlessness move you,*
> *You lose touch with who you are.*
>
> — Lao-Tzu

Question Everything

So often we do things in a particular way because that's the way we learned to do it, and we never question it. You may have heard this story, but it's worth retelling: A husband watched as his newly-wed wife prepared a roast for cooking and he asked, "Why do you cut off the ends?" to which she replied, "I don't know. That's how my mother does it." So the next time the young man saw his mother-in-law, he asked her, "When you are preparing a roast, why do you cut off the ends?" to which she replied, "I don't know. That's how my mother always does it." Curious now, she decided to call her mother. She asked, "Mom, when you are preparing a roast, why do you cut off the ends?" to which her mother replied, "Because that's the only way to make it fit in my roasting pan!"

Ask yourself: Am I doing things *my* way, for *my* own reasons, or because that's what everyone else is doing?

WHO ARE YOU REALLY?

In *Live Your Dream,* author Joyce Chapman encourages us to pay conscious attention to what we are thinking and doing as a tool for questioning and ultimately understanding who we really are "beneath all the shoulds, buts, and external influences." Chapman suggests that you notice:

- Your first thought when waking up
- As you prepare for the day, whether you are excited or dreading it
- Whether you look for the good or focus on the problem
- The most important part of your day and the most enjoyable
- What it is that you willingly set aside everything else to do
- The kind of people you hang out with and how you feel around them (alive or bored, for example)
- Whom you're attracted to and why
- Whom you try to impress
- How you feel when someone asks you what work you do
- Moments when you feel fully alive
- What you keep putting off
- What you appreciate
- What you remembered, and what you forgot
- Whom you put first and last

Look inside. Take a personal retreat in which you devote a few hours or even a day or two — perhaps with a few friends — to talk about your sense of purpose in life and how you want to spend your time here on earth. If you were to die tomorrow, what would you like to be remembered for? What personal qualities? What achievements? Most of us are moving so quickly each day that we don't stop to think about where we are going or what we are doing. But stopping and thinking can change your life.

Freeze your commitments. Don't take on anything new right now. Plan to spend some time getting to know yourself. Who are you? What do your choices in life (career, home, car, clothes, and friends) say about you? Is that who you really are? For example, if it didn't matter what anyone else thought about what kind of car you drive, what kind of car would you drive? If you believe that what other people say or think about you matters, ask yourself why. Why is it so important to you?

Ask yourself, "Who am I?" Try to base your answer not on what you have done or who you have been in the past or who you will be in the future but on who you are right now. Can you do it? Our perceptions of ourselves are very often clouded by past experiences and future assumptions that can prevent us from discovering who we really are.

Evaluate Your Values and Beliefs

What would you like to have more of in your life and why? What would you like to have less of and why? What motivates you? Is it money? Money for what? Is it time? Time for what?

When you know what motivates you, you can build motivators into your life as a reward for achieving milestones. You might take a day off to go to the beach, hire a housekeeper, or throw a party.

What do you value? According to Joyce Chapman in *Live Your Dream,* to determine what's important to you, look at the life you are living now and answer the following questions:

- What do you find yourself doing most often?
- How do you spend your time?
- What do you talk about?
- What do you do when you have a day off?
- What offends your sense of justice and provokes outrage in you?
- Which of your values are you most proud of?

Remember that life is a journey, not a destination. You are in the driver's seat. Where would you like to go next? What do you hope to accomplish in your life? Is what you're doing now helping you to achieve your goals? What would be your ideal day? Your ideal week? Your ideal year? What do your answers tell you about yourself?

Make a list of your values. These are the qualities you admire and respect in yourself and others. Honesty, resourcefulness, intelligence, style, and simplicity are just a few examples. Identify your values by looking at the "whys" behind how you spend your time and money.

> *A human being*
> *Fashions his consequences*
> *As surely as he fashions*
> *His goods or his dwelling.*
> *Nothing he says,*
> *Thinks or does*
> *Is without consequences.*
>
> — Norman Cousins

Imagine that you have only a short time to live. In *Live Your Dream,* Joyce Chapman suggests this exercise: Think back over the past month. How would you spend your time differently? How would your priorities change? What would become more (or less) important to you?

Become aware of what you believe. Positive beliefs drive positive behaviors; negative beliefs drive negative behaviors. If you are unhappy with your behavior, try to determine what belief is prompting it, and then take the necessary steps to replace that belief with a more positive one. For example, if you want to lose weight because your clothes are getting uncomfortable but you don't change your eating or exercise habits, perhaps you believe that you don't deserve to feel good. To change your behavior, you've got to change that belief.

Commit to Change

Embrace change. Recognize that change is a natural process of life. Like every other creature on earth, we have the ability to adapt ourselves to our environment. We can choose to make positive changes in ourselves that will improve our quality of life.

Allow time to change. Focus on the process of changing rather than the outcome of change. Be patient.

> *No one can make you change.*
> *No one can stop you from changing.*
> *No one really knows how*
> *you must change.*
> *Not even you.*
> *Not until you start.*
>
> — David Viscott

Change one thing. Choose one value or quality or characteristic you would like to develop — or one you would like to eliminate. List all the ways you can think of to do that. Start doing one of these things today.

Create imaginary allies. In *Live the Life You Love,* Barbara Sher advises us to gather our allies. She says, "... the unknown can be frightening... you need to know you're not alone... [and] have a support team." She suggests creating a team of imaginary spirit allies: for example, a person in history, someone from your childhood, a fictional character. Imagine what advice they would give if you asked for their support.

Reclaim the power of choice. When you let someone else make choices for you, you are giving up the power to make yourself happy. Reclaim that power and all the happiness that is rightfully yours.

Just *don't* do it. Stopping *is* an option. If the reason you continue to do something is that you've been doing it for a while and feel it would be time and energy wasted to stop now, think again. Think about what you have gained and how you have grown through your investment of time, energy, and money. Now think about the time, energy, or money you are wasting by continuing to do something simply because you feel obligated to do it. Think, too, about all the things you could be doing but can't do because of this obligation. If you are unhappy, unfulfilled, or unsatisfied, give yourself permission to leave this thing behind and move on.

Give it a try. Be willing to try something new to see how it works. If you keep doing things the same way, you'll keep getting the same results.

Commit to your goal. The moment you fully commit to a goal is the moment when that goal begins to be a reality. Without full commitment, a goal is just a goal.

To change your life, follow the advice of Dr. William James, the founder of modern psychology:

- Start immediately.
- Do it flamboyantly.
- Make no exceptions.

Create a New Vision

Once you've determined your beliefs and values, you are ready to put them into action. Don't be afraid to let the world see who you really are. When you "be yourself," you give others permission to do the same. With no false fronts to keep up, life is so much simpler and more satisfying.

Start by developing a vision statement. A vision statement is a statement about what you want to be and what you want to achieve or contribute. Take some time to develop it. Write it down. Keep it where you will see it frequently. Read it aloud.

Make a list of things that make you happy. Challenge yourself to come up with at least 100 ideas. Then resolve to do at least three of those things each day for the next three weeks.

Choose your beliefs. If you believe that you are a capable, talented person, then you will become that person. If you believe that people are helpful, you will find yourself in the company of helpful people. What you believe about yourself and your life will become true. You might feel that you are only acting or pretending, but faking it is the easiest way to change your life. Fake it until you can make it.

Hold mental rehearsals. Visualize yourself reaching your goal, or visualize yourself going through the steps to reach that goal.

Develop affirmations. An affirmation is a positive statement that often begins with the words *I will* or *I can* or *I am*. An example of an affirmation for a cancer patient is: "I can feel myself growing healthier and stronger each day." Write several affirmations and post them somewhere as a reminder to say them aloud every day. The power of affirmations does not come from writing or reading them, but from the vibrations of saying them aloud.

Surround yourself with inspiration. Find quotes or sayings or posters with messages that inspire you to be and do your best. Place them where you will see them every day.

SHOULD YOU?

Eliminate the words *should* and *have to* from your vocabulary and your mind. Replace these words with "want" and "choose to" and apply them. If you really don't believe that you want or choose to do something, then why are you doing it? Consider eliminating such activities from your life.

Express your values through your actions. Once you are aware of your values, consciously choose to inject them into your life. For example, if you value integrity, make only those promises you can keep — and keep them.

Keep focused on your values. Take 10 minutes each day for quiet time to reflect on how you will (or did) align your expenditures of time, energy, and money with your values throughout the day.

Live with no regrets. If you were to die tomorrow, what would you regret not having done? How can you live your life today (and every day) so that you will have no regrets?

Be gentle with yourself. If you find yourself slipping back into old patterns, congratulate yourself for recognizing that! Then reclaim your will and move on.

Finding Your Balance

Everything in moderation — that's the secret to happiness and good health, right? Right. So why is it so difficult to maintain balance in our lives? Because maintaining balance takes concentration and effort.

And how do you know when your life is in balance? When you function as well when things are going bad as when things are going good and your overall satisfaction with life remains the same.

Bring balance to your life by focusing attention where attention is needed. The next time you feel angry, frustrated, guilty, resentful, or stressed, note whether it is about home issues, career issues, or leisure time. Do you frequently feel this way about this area of your life? If so, resolve to bring your attention to this area and make an effort to make some changes that will bring balance into your life.

Identify What's Important

Are you a hard worker or a workaholic? The difference between them is state of mind. Working hard to achieve a goal is admirable. Workaholics work for the sake of working in the belief that it will somehow make them worthier.

Imagine life as a game in which you are juggling five balls. Name them: work, family, health, friends, spirit. Work is a rubber ball; if you drop it, it will bounce back. But the other four balls — family, health, friends, and spirit — are made of glass. If you drop one of these, it might be irrevocably damaged.

Focus on one thing at a time. When you are with your family, give them 100 percent of your attention and energy. When you are at work, engage fully in your job. And when you are playing, have fun!

Learn to Relax

It's okay to stop and rest. If your life is a whirlwind of activity seven days a week, try balancing it with some true leisure time — a time to just sit — without feeling the need to be productive or busy doing something. Spend less time talking about your need to relax and more time doing it. It will refresh your spirit and make you more efficient when you return to your responsibilities.

Take it easy. If you work particularly long and hard one day or if you feel exhausted, make a conscious effort to take it a little easier the next day. Sleep later if you can. Go out to lunch with a friend. Leave work a half hour early (or at least on time). Squeeze in a nap. Put your feet up and read a book. Or do nothing at all. The key is to *relax and recharge.*

PROGRESSIVE RELAXATION EXERCISE

To give yourself a time-out, try this relaxing and refreshing exercise.

Put on some relaxing music and then set a timer for 20 minutes or so. Lie flat on your back on a carpeted floor or mat. Take a deep breath in, and slowly let it out. Continue to breathe deeply. Follow each breath with your mind; really focus on each inhalation and exhalation. Let yourself relax into each breath. Relax your feet. Imagine that they are growing very heavy and that the feeling of heaviness is spreading very slowly through your body, from your toes, up through your legs, to your hips and lower back, chest and shoulders, and arms and hands. Even your face feels heavy, as if gravity is pulling it down into the floor. Just lie there, enjoying the stillness of the moment. When the timer goes off, slowly deepen your breaths and begin to stretch. Roll onto one side for a minute, and then sit up slowly.

Breathe to the power of 10. When you find your-self clenching your teeth or tightening up in response to a stressor, take a deep breath to the count of 10 and exhale to the count of 10. Repeat several times.

Change up. A change from your regular routine can be just as relaxing as a rest — maybe even more restful if you're the type that finds it hard to sit still. Try doing something you really love to do, but haven't done in a long while.

Take a day off. If you've been swamped with deadlines, spend a whole day with no plans. Just do what you feel like doing, when you feel like doing it. If you have to make a lot of decisions at work, give yourself a time-out: Let someone else decide where to go, what to do, and what to eat. If your job requires constant contact with people, escape into solitude. Go for a walk in the woods or paddle a canoe on a quiet lake.

Putting It into Practice

If you wish you had more time for your family, then make more time. Where there's a will, there's a way. Perhaps you can:

- Cut back on work hours.
- Change jobs.
- Trade full-time for part-time work.
- Work at home one or more days a week.

- Cut your commuting time by working closer to home.
- Ask for help. Many employers are responding to the pressure on today's workers with benefits like flexible scheduling, job sharing, work-at-home arrangements, and even counseling.

Watch your speed. If you have a tendency to drive faster than the speed limit, get in the habit of allowing an additional 5 to 10 minutes of driving time. You'll be not only less stressed, but safer too. And so will everyone around you.

Pace yourself. If you are feeling the stress of being on the go all day long, examine your schedule. Is there a commitment you can forgo? Or is there someone else who can do some of the things you are doing to free up some of your time?

Schedule free time into your day. Free time is time to enjoy activities that you really enjoy. Plan to do something you love to do every day — anything from playing solitaire on your computer to reading or drawing to walking the dog.

Detach yourself slightly from your environment. Use this as a technique for becoming more objective about your role at home and work. As a more objective observer, you are more likely to find ways to improve your balance.

Delegate. Have too much "home" work and not enough fun? List daily and weekly jobs at home. Give some of your jobs to family members who are able to help.

Schedule time for fun. At the beginning of each month, put "fun stuff to do" on your calendar to balance the demands and responsibilities of home and career. Include family events as well as things that will give you private time.

BALANCING FAMILY AND FRIENDS

Just because you have a family doesn't mean you have to give up your friends. Instead of always trying to schedule separate time, unite the three Fs: family, friends, and fun. Choose activities that everyone — even friends without children — can enjoy.

- Attend a sporting event.
- Go to a water park.
- Take a hike.
- Rent boats or canoes on a nearby lake.
- Go camping for a weekend.
- Go skiing or cycling.
- Have a picnic at the beach.
- Make plans to go on vacation together.
- Celebrate the holidays together.

Be flexible with your schedule. Don't try to plan every minute of your time. Leave time to do whatever you feel like doing at the moment, which may be nothing at all.

Take a problem out to lunch. Sometimes our best efforts are thwarted by people who don't necessarily mean to trip us up but they do. For example, you may be doing great work on the job, but someone else keeps taking all the credit. Once a month, take your number one "human problem" out to breakfast or lunch and frankly discuss what's bothering you. Keep the conversation focused not on the person's behavior but on how that behavior makes you feel.

Follow Your Passion

In this chapter . . .

- *Believe in Yourself*
- *Identify Your Gifts*
- *Go For It*
- *What's Stopping You?*
- *Working for Yourself*

In chapter one, you learned how putting yourself first helps you become a stronger, healthier person. In chapter two, you learned how important it is to be yourself and to let decisions flow naturally from your values and beliefs. In this chapter, what you will learn is how to follow your passion to a more fulfilling life.

Very often, feelings of discontent stem from what we do for a living because, in America anyway, who we are is so closely tied to what we do. If we're unhappy about our life's work, we are unhappy with our lives.

If you're working full time, you spend about half of your waking hours at work during a typical week. That's a lot of time. Do you love what you're doing or do you dread going in to work each day?

Does your work energize or drain you? If you don't like what you do for a living, your dissatisfaction naturally spreads into other areas of your life, creating unhappiness there too.

More often than not, when you talk to someone who really enjoys her job, you will learn that she is not doing the job she initially set out to do. But somehow, someway, she figured out what kind of work would bring her the greatest satisfaction. And there's usually a pretty inspiring story to go along with it. You'll read three such stories in this chapter.

People who love what they do are no more special or gifted than you. The only difference is that they dared to follow their passion. You, too, are free to discover and pursue what brings a sense of purpose, satisfaction, and happiness to your life. And truly, the only person stopping you is you.

Believe in Yourself

When we were little kids, we thought we could do anything and be anybody when we grew up. Somewhere along the way we lost faith in ourselves. But faith is where the path to satisfaction starts, so teach yourself to believe again — starting right now.

Go with your gut. Have you ever had a gut feeling that was so strong you just had to go with it? It turned out to be the best thing you could have done, didn't it? Let your instincts guide you.

Don't underestimate your worth. The next time you start to compare yourself to someone you think is brighter, prettier, worthier, or whatever, stop. You are who you are — a very unique and special individual. Believe in yourself. That's all that really matters.

Listen to your dreams. One of the ways your inner wisdom speaks to you is through dreams, especially when you are working through a difficult situation or trying to find a solution to a problem. Sometimes your dreams are your unconscious trying to help you. Look for the helping message in your dreams.

Give it your best shot. Whether you are trying to lose weight, launch a new career, or save a faltering marriage, try your best. If it doesn't work out, you can be secure in the knowledge that you did everything within your power and your ability. Remember that nothing worth doing is easy.

Act as if you can do whatever you want to do and eventually you will be able to do it.

> *It takes courage to grow up and turn out to be who you really are.*
>
> — e. e. cummings

Revel in your accomplishments. Accept praise for a job well done. Really let it sink in and become a part of who you are — don't just brush it off in modesty. On momentous occasions, write down your thoughts and feelings about your achievements to reread on a day when you're feeling down.

Remember the three Rs:

- Respect for self
- Respect for others
- Responsibility for all your actions

Appreciate and accept yourself. If you do, others will too.

Keep pushing forward. Don't give up as long as you still have something to give. Nothing is really over until you stop trying.

Don't be afraid to admit a mistake. Being less than perfect is the common thread of humanity. When you realize that you've made a mistake, take immediate steps to correct it.

Accept your emotions. It's okay to feel sad or angry. It's okay to cry. Part of believing in yourself is accepting your feelings. To deny your feelings is to deny yourself.

Be your own best friend. Eleanor Roosevelt wrote, "Friendship with oneself is all-important, because without it one cannot be friends with anyone else in the world."

Identify Your Gifts

We all are born with special talents or gifts. Your gifts might include compassion, humor, insight, or inspiring others. Or you may be a born comedian or a natural peacemaker. In *Live the Life You Love,* Barbara Sher suggests that you think about everything you have ever enjoyed doing: "If you base what you do on your gifts, you will be unusually good at it." Identify your natural gifts — and use them.

Don't let others limit you with their expectations. Make decisions based on what you know will bring you joy. Only *you* can determine what will bring joy to your life.

What do you love to do? What makes you happy to be alive? If your time and money were unlimited, and you could do anything you wanted, what would you do? Recognizing the things that give you joy and satisfaction — and increasing the amount of time you spend doing them — puts you on the path to increased happiness and fulfillment.

Step back and see yourself through another set of eyes. Pretend that you are someone who has just met you. What desirable qualities might this person you've just created see in you?

D₀ what you are. "By unlocking the secrets of your personality type, you *can* find a truly fulfilling job that enhances the quality of your life," say Paul D. Tieger and Barbara Barron-Tieger, authors of the book *Do What You Are*. Based on a scientific approach to categorizing personalities into 16 distinct types, the book is a wonderful resource for helping you match your personality to a satisfying and rewarding career.

WHAT ARE YOUR S.W.O.T.s?

Businesspeople often analyze the viability of ideas and develop strategies based on the S.W.O.T. technique. Try it as a tool for assessing your own goals.

- **Strengths.** What strengths do you possess that will enable you to succeed? List your talents and skills.
- **Weaknesses.** Identify your weaknesses. What can you do to shore up these weaknesses? Develop and implement a plan of action.
- **Opportunities.** What is going on in the world around you? Can you see any trends? Where is the greatest need for your expertise or talent?
- **Threats.** What obstacles stand in your way? How big a threat are these obstacles to your success? What can you do to minimize or steer around these obstacles?

Don't confuse skills with talents. Look not at what you *can* do but at what you *want* to do. We develop abilities because they are useful. For example, you may have learned how to do your current job very well, but that doesn't mean it's what you want to do. If you do a job because that's what you know how to do and not because you want to do it, you are likely to be very unhappy.

Close your eyes and visualize yourself working at your dream job. In what type of environment are you working? What kind of people are you working with and what sort of interaction do you have with them? The more vivid you can make your vision, the more it will help to clarify your dream.

Don't Just Dream It, Live It!

Think back to your childhood. What did you want to be when you grew up? What kind of response did you get from your parents or teachers? Often, we don't pursue our original passion because of negative feedback we received at a tender age. For example, you might have wanted to be an astronaut, but your parents told you that you didn't do well enough in science or math. What if your dream was to be a superhero? Well, obviously you can't become a comic-book hero. What was it about being a superhero that turned you on? Did you like the thought of rescuing people from danger or simply being of service? There are many ways to live a life of service.

> *There is only one success — to spend*
> *your life your way.*
>
> — Christopher Morley

PROFILE OF SUCCESS

Profile of Success: Helen Volk
Former Occupation: Attorney
Current Occupation: Founder and president of Beyond Clutter, professional organizer, speaker, writer

Helen Volk practiced law for 17 years. Now she helps people de-clutter and de-stress their lives. Helen, who used to be a pack rat herself, believes that you have to empty your life to fulfill it. That's what she did. She downsized by giving away two thirds of her possessions and moving to a smaller house. "[I realized one day that] not one religious tradition teaches that the purpose of life is owning stuff. But they all stress simple living as a spiritual principle. It was a revelation that shook me to the core of my being," says Helen. Once she committed to the idea of simplifying her life, the rest was easy. Now, through workshops, seminars, and one-on-one sessions, Helen teaches others that they can enjoy fuller, more meaningful lives and feel richer than ever by having less.

Dream your dream. In *How Much Joy Can You Stand?*, Suzanne Falter-Barns says, "Dream your dream, and then dare to stake claim in it. What you will receive in return will be all the riches of the world — yourself, as originally intended."

Make a dream board. One idea from the book *Live Your Dream* is to cut out magazine pictures and words, use photos, or draw illustrations that portray your dream of who you want to be. Include the aspects of life such as family, friends, and accomplishments that are important to you. In essence, what you design is an advertisement for the life you want to live. Put this dream board where you will see it every day.

Go For It

How do you know if what you want is what will make you happy? There is only one way to know for sure: Go for it. Allowing yourself to follow your true passion will not only enhance your life, it will also give you the sense of accomplishment that comes from taking action.

Start Small

Leverage your talents. Look for career opportunities that enable you to use your inherent skills. If you are a natural problem-solver, for instance, make up a list of occupations that require problem-solving. Yes, it's going to be a long list! Spend some time visualizing yourself in each one of these occupations. Do any of them excite you? Spend a few days or more "noodling" with the idea of this or that career. Then start researching what kind of qualifications you will need for the careers that most appeal to you.

Inch your way to your dream career. To get through the front door, you may need specific education and experience. But if you're lacking these, don't despair. Perhaps there is a side door. Identify the industry in which you wish to work. Is there another job within that field for which you may be qualified? Once you are there, you can take the necessary steps to prove yourself.

Rewrite your résumé to call attention to your natural talents. Start by redefining your objective. What do you want in your next job? Write up your experience in a way that highlights your natural gifts and supports your objective. Don't hesitate to hire a professional résumé writer if you find that you are unable to do this yourself.

Look around you. Perhaps your dream job is not as far away as you think. If you are currently employed, is there some way of altering or adding to your current job responsibilities to make better use of your talents while still serving your employer? Think about it.

Be patient. Know that every action, every step you take is bringing you one step closer to your dream career.

Just do it. Don't waste your life waiting for the perfect moment to begin something you want to do. The perfect time is now.

Putting Goals into Action

Break goals into mini goals. In *Life Mapping,* author Bill Cohen suggests dividing your goals into a list of activities necessary to complete those goals. Keep breaking them into smaller and smaller activities, until each individual activity can be completed within a week or a day. Take this list and put it in chronological order (what you need to do this week, next week, and so on). Then get going on what you need to do this week.

MAKE LIGHT OF YOUR WORK

If you dread doing some of the things on your goals list, try to make them fun. Author Bill Cohen suggests, for example, that if you have to call a long list of people, try to make each of them laugh, and keep a tally.

Write down 100 things you'd like to do before you die. Identify the top 10 and work them into your goals. Then determine which ones you want to accomplish this year.

Talk to people who are doing what you want to do. Call or write and ask for an information interview. Tell them that you simply want them to talk about their work. Ask them how they got started, what they think it takes to succeed in this business, and anything else you want to know.

Seek out a mentor. Many senior-level individuals are willing to make time for people who take the initiative to seek them out. Start by offering to buy lunch for that person. Use this time to present one or two of your ideas or challenges. Then listen to the voice of experience.

Put first things first. Let's say that you want to start your own business and you have established this as your top priority. Perhaps one of the challenges you face is saving enough money so that you can quit your job. You've been trying, but there is never enough left over at the end of the month. Try paying yourself first. Out of each paycheck, before you pay anyone else, set aside a sum of money for yourself. This is the amount you would normally fritter away over the course of a month. By securing it for yourself, you are securing your future.

Volunteer your services. One of the best and quickest ways to gain experience and make yourself known is to offer your services on a volunteer basis. Organizations are *always* looking for people who are willing to help! For example, if you want to be a writer, volunteer to write an organization's newsletter. If you want to get involved in politics, join an election committee. Not only will you get experience, you also will meet the "movers and shakers" in your intended line of work.

Be willing to learn what you need to know. Read every book you can find on the subject of your passion. Take a crash course. Research the industry. Talk to experts.

Hold on to your values. Following your passion may be a stretch — financially, emotionally, physically, and intellectually — but it should never require you to compromise your values. If something doesn't feel right, it's not right for you. Walk away.

Work every day toward your goal. If you want to change careers, do something every day to work toward achieving your goal of a new career. Make a phone call. Write a letter. Practice your craft. Network. Join an association or organization for people who do what you want to do.

> *Desire is the key to motivation,
> but it's your determination and
> commitment to a goal — your
> commitment to excellence — that will
> enable you to attain the success you seek.*
>
> — Mario Andretti

PROFILE OF SUCCESS

Profile of Success: W. Bradford Swift
Former Occupation: Veterinarian
Current Occupation: Founder and
director of Life On Purpose Institute,
life purpose coach, author, and speaker

Brad Swift left behind a successful veterinary practice to pursue a passion for writing, which he later discovered was simply an extension of his true purpose. He says, "[It was] during a spiritual retreat that my reason for being on the Earth became clear. It was to serve others by helping them gain clarity about their life purpose." Brad founded the Life On Purpose Institute, an organization whose mission mirrors Brad's: to live a purposeful and passionate life of service, mindful and abundant simplicity, and spiritual serenity. Brad now helps others clarify their life purpose and live true to it: "From living on purpose, I've been blessed with an extraordinary life in which I am satisfied and fulfilled."

What's Stopping You?

You've identified your talents. You've found your true calling. You've researched the best way to pursue it. So what's holding you back? Fear and uncertainty are usually the main obstacles on the road to self-fulfillment. Just remember that there is nothing wrong with being afraid — but you *can* learn to overcome this feeling.

Confront Your Fear

Don't be afraid to fail. You fell down the first time you tried to walk, but you didn't let that stop you from trying again. Were you able to swim or ride a bike on your first try? Probably not. In failing, we learn what doesn't work, which frees us to try various other approaches that might work — until we finally succeed. The only real failure is not trying at all.

Never say no to yourself. Callie Khouri, the screenwriter who wrote *Thelma & Louise,* had always wanted to write but lacked the confidence to try. One night, while sitting in her car, the idea for *Thelma & Louise* hit her like a brick. Although she had never attended film school, she decided not to give in to her usual self-doubt because along with the movie idea came a feeling of release: "I am not going to say no to myself anymore." The movie became a box-office smash and today Callie Khouri is a full-time professional screenwriter.

Be brave. What's the worst possible thing that could happen? This is an excellent question to ask yourself when you are faced with a difficult decision or you are afraid to do something.

> *Whatever you can do or dream you can, begin it. Boldness has beauty, power, and magic in it.*
>
> — Johann Wolfgang von Goethe

If you're scared, do it scared! We're all afraid of doing things we've never done before; it's only natural. Here's a little secret: Once you do it, you won't be so afraid the second time around.

Do a little each day. If you can't muster enough courage or if you need more preparation before you try, take it a step at a time. For example, if you want to become writer, set aside at least 15 minutes a day to write. It doesn't matter what you write and it doesn't have to be good. After a month or two, select something you've written and submit it to a magazine or publisher. If it gets rejected, don't take it personally. Submit the same piece to someone else or a new piece to the same person. Meanwhile, read up on what it takes to become a successful writer. Remember, all good writers were beginners at one time, and most of them still have the rejection letters to prove it!

Worry about today's problems, not tomorrow's problems. There's a famous old southern expression: Don't worry that the mule is blind — just load the wagon.

When you lose, don't lose the lesson. Learn from your mistakes. We learn far more from our mistakes than from our successes.

REMOVING OBSTACLES

Do you want to make your dream a reality? Write down all of the stumbling blocks that are keeping you from pursuing this dream. Now look at each one of these reasons and ask yourself, "Is this within my power to change? What could I do to change this?" Write down every answer you can think of, including outrageous answers like "win the lottery" and "have my own talk show." When you are finished, review your answers and choose the three that are most feasible. Of these three things, choose one that you can start working on today, and work on it every day. Achieving your dream is like trying to move a large boulder down an incline. It's hard work to get it rolling, but once it starts, it quickly gathers speed and momentum in the right direction.

> *We make a living by what we get,*
> *we make a life by what we give.*
>
> — Winston Churchill

Make a list. *Live Your Dream* author Joyce Chapman suggests listing 20 habits and/or beliefs that you allow to stand in the way of achieving your dream. Procrastination and overcommitting are two examples of dream-defeating *habits;* believing that you're not qualified enough or smart enough is a dream-defeating *belief.* Next to each item on your list, write a new habit or belief to replace the old one. You might also want to include on your list people who stand in your way, but instead of replacing them, consider how you might modify your relationship with them.

Accept responsibility for your own success. There's only one person who can make you successful and happy and that's you.

Stop making excuses. It's only natural to have some doubts and concerns about following your passion, particularly if it means changing careers and *especially* if you have a family to support. Think you're too old or it's too late? Apparently Grandma Moses thought differently. She began painting in her late 70s. Think you don't have time to pursue your passion? You can always make time for what's really important by spending less time on less important things.

PROFILE OF SUCCESS

Profile of Success: Judith Warnke
Former Occupation: Registered nurse
Current Occupation: Licensed massage therapist and certified Kripalu yoga instructor

After being diagnosed with fibromyalgia, Judi Warnke was determined to get her life back. She adjusted her diet, quit smoking, and started exercising. Then she discovered — almost simultaneously — massage and yoga, which she describes as "the great Aha!" During a meditation at a life-in-transformation workshop, Judi realized with no uncertainty and no hesitation that she wanted to make an exit from her 20-year nursing career and become a yoga instructor and a massage therapist. She said, "It came to me like a flashing neon sign that said: *Walk this way.*"

Through massage therapy and yoga, Judi has healed herself and now extends her energy to empower other people to heal themselves. When asked what she loves best about what she does, Judi says, "There's no distinction between who I am and what I do. My work is clearly and completely an extension of me."

Working for Yourself

Self-employment is a dream that many people share, especially if it means working from home. For some people, that's all it is: a dream. Others find the courage to try it, but discover that they were happier with a steady paycheck. Still others couldn't imagine ever going back to a regular job. A little bit of careful thought up front can help you determine if self-employment is right for you.

When is the best time to start your own business? Some say that you should wait until you have so much money that it doesn't matter if you lose it — or start up when you have so little, you have nothing to lose. But don't let money be the deciding factor. People who do what they love quickly discover that the money becomes a by-product of their passion. Focus all your time and energy on working to the best of your ability. The money will come.

Take a Reality Check

Make sure you understand the realities of self-employment. For example, working for yourself often means working *by* yourself, and that can get pretty lonely. It also requires a tremendous amount of self-discipline. You've got to get up and get going every day. The more you can stick to a regular routine, the more successful you are likely to be.

Be honest with yourself. How much time are you willing to commit? What are you willing to do? What are you willing to give up and for how long?

Face the facts. If you tell yourself that you want your own business but never do anything about it, what does that tell you? Is it really what you want? If so, commit to it and take action. If not, try to figure out what it is about self-employment that appeals to you. For example, if you like the idea of having more freedom, perhaps you can negotiate to work at home one day a week.

INSURE YOURSELF

One of the biggest challenges in becoming self-employed is finding a health insurance plan. But if you do a little research, you will find that you can obtain affordable insurance for yourself and your family. The easiest, but not necessarily least expensive, way to keep your coverage in effect is to pick up the premiums on your current employer's health insurance plan.

Shop around. Look for organizations and associations that offer group insurance for their members. Start with the organizations to which you currently belong and those you might be interested in joining. Check out your local chamber of commerce and the United States Federation of Small Businesses. Keep in mind that the more members an organization has, the less expensive its health insurance premiums will be. You will need to pay an annual fee to belong to the organization, as well as your insurance premium.

Start part time or freelance. Before you quit your day job, try starting your business on a part-time or freelance basis. It's a great way to get a feel for the marketplace and your ability to make it on your own. Eventually, you will reach a point where you will have enough confidence (and income) to make it a full-time venture — or you will decide that it's not right for you.

Interview self-employed people. Talk to people who are currently self-employed — ideally, people who are in your line of work — to find out if self-employment is right for you.

WORK OPPORTUNITIES
FOR STAY-AT-HOME PARENTS

If your passion is to be at home with your children but you need to supplement your family income, think about how you could do that from home. Is the work you do now something you could do from home? Do you have a professional skill such as writing, typing, accounting, or bookkeeping that could be promoted as a service? Can you turn a hobby or a talent into an income producer? A great place to start looking for information and help on home work opportunities is www.miserly-moms.com, where you will find a special list of links for work-at-home-moms (WAHM) sites.

Promote yourself. Don't think that just because you're in business, customers are going to come knocking on your door. There are many excellent books on ways to promote your business on a shoestring budget. One of the best ways to get your name known is to volunteer your expertise in a high-profile position in one or more industry or trade associations. Also look for networking organizations through which members regularly meet to share leads.

> *Your talent is God's gift to you.*
> *What you do with it*
> *is your gift back to God.*
>
> — Leo Buscaglia

Be prepared to wear many hats. Regardless of your profession or trade, working for yourself usually means that you are also the secretary, bookkeeper, salesperson, and janitor. And that requires good time-management skills. Consider taking a course or reading up on time-management techniques.

Give yourself a start-up cushion. When starting a business, it's always a good idea to have enough money in the bank to cover your expenses for at least six months. Alternatively, have a backup plan (such as waiting on tables, housecleaning, or temporary work) that will allow you to earn enough to pay the bills.

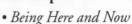

Live Mindfully

In this chapter . . .

- *Being Here and Now*
- *Cultivating Mindfulness*
- *Nurturing Relationships*
- *Fostering Love*
- *Caring for Family*
- *Mindfulness in the 21st Century*

M indfulness is about waking up, living in the present, and making conscious choices about what you do, say, and think. Your future will be determined by the choices you make now. Choosing well — in every moment — takes constant watchfulness. But it is time well spent.

Also known as conscious living, mindfulness can alleviate stress and dramatically improve your relationships with yourself, loved ones, and the world. Being mindful is being attentive and aware. The opposite of mindfulness is mindlessness or ignorance. Which do you prefer?

Being Here and Now

When you're traveling at warp speed, as so many of us do (on autopilot, no less), you tend not to think much about what you're doing in and with your life. In the "busyness" of living, we lose ourselves as well as the precious moments of time. But our time on earth is the only time we have! When you concentrate on being fully present in the moment, the moments accumulate over months and years into a life well lived.

Begin Right Now

Don't just do something, sit there. Take time now to look at what's going on around you. What do you see and hear? What do you feel? Stopping every once in a while makes you more aware of what you are doing when you start moving again.

Worry about right now. If you find yourself worrying about something that might happen tomorrow or some day, concentrate on today. Take it one day at a time. And if that's too much to think about, take it one hour at a time.

> *Yesterday is history, tomorrow is a mystery, and today is a gift. That's why it is called the present.*
>
> — Anonymous

Leave the past behind. When your mind is cluttered with past experiences, especially negative ones, it drains energy and productivity from today. Repeat to yourself as often as needed each day: Where am I? Here. What time is it? Now.

Focus on the task at hand. Whether you are washing dishes, driving to the store, doing your job, or helping your children with homework, focus all of your attention and energy on what you are doing.

Cultivating Mindfulness

Despite the seeming simplicity, it's not easy to "stop and smell the roses." The fact is that we've trained ourselves to be constantly on the go, to always be doing *something* and thinking ahead. But if you never live in and fully enjoy the present, what kind of life are you living? How much are you missing out on?

Practice Awareness

Slow down. Try this simple exercise: Stand up and deliberately move across the room in slow motion. Notice how it increases your awareness and expands time. That's what slowing down in life can do for you.

Watch your every move. Over the next week, before you do anything, ask yourself *why* you are doing it. Is it important? Is it important enough to do right now? A ringing telephone is a perfect example. Most people automatically answer the phone without *deciding* to answer it. It's there for our convenience, but how easy it is to become enslaved by it! How much of what you do is action and how much is *re*action? By paying closer attention to what you are doing, you can make more conscious choices about how you spend your time.

> *It's only possible to live happily ever after on a moment-to-moment basis.*
>
> — Margaret Bonnano

Take a hike. A long stroll is the perfect opportunity to reflect on what's happening in the world and in your life.

Set your own goals. Think about what you want in life and what you need to do to make your life the way you want it. Write down your goals as they occur to you. Cross off your list any goals that are imposed on you by someone else.

Listen to Yourself

Listen to your thoughts. Don't judge them; just recognize and accept them. To help stay focused, you might even try to visualize your thoughts in a cloud.

Listen to what you say. How often do you think or say, "I have to"? Replace this statement with "I choose to." It will relieve a lot of the pressure you place on yourself. And it will give you a whole new perspective.

Look at where you spend your time and energy. Many times, we focus our energy, time, and attention on trivial matters to avoid dealing with larger, more important issues. A preoccupation with keeping a spotless house, for example, may be masking a communication problem in your marriage.

EATING MINDFULLY

Make it a point to sit down when you eat. When eating, be mindful (or aware) of each mouthful of food. Notice the texture as well as the taste. Chew slowly, savoring the flavor. Put down your fork between each mouthful. Eating more mindfully allows us to more fully enjoy our food and aids proper digestion. In addition, eating slowly gives our stomachs time to register the feeling of fullness, which reduces overeating.

If you often overeat, ask yourself why. Are you using food as a drug? To reward yourself? To fill a void? To cope with emotions or escape from life's problems? Try to get in touch with the real reason you overeat. It might be helpful to see a counselor who can help you sort it out. Once you know *why* you are overeating, you can begin to feed the real need within you.

Get in touch with your emotions. Crying doesn't always mean you're sad. Sometimes we cry out of joy. Or we cry out of anger and frustration. And sometimes we take out our anger on people and things that are not at all our real targets. Ask yourself at regular intervals throughout the day: How am I feeling? What do I need? If you're reacting because you're tired, take a nap. If you want to unwind, call a friend. If you're stressed out, do some deep breathing.

ELIMINATE MENTAL CLUTTER THROUGH MEDITATION

A lot of stress can be traced to the negative "chatter" that goes on in our minds — muddled thoughts about what we said or did or should have said or done, or what we think we might say or do — which only serves to distract us from fully enjoying the present. Meditation provides a welcome break from internal as well as external noise. Try this exercise, one of many ways to meditate:

1. Sit quietly in a chair or on the floor and gently close your eyes. Bring mindful awareness to your breath as it flows in and out of your body. Is it shallow or deep? Is your inhale longer, shorter, or the same as your exhale? Just notice these things without changing them.

2. Pay attention to the sensations in your body as you breathe — the feel of your breath in your nostrils, your lungs, and your belly.

3. Allow yourself to experience whatever feelings come up. If stray thoughts about the past or future enter your mind, exhale them with your next breath and continue to focus on your breathing and this moment.

4. Do this for at least 5 minutes and try to work up to 15 to 20 minutes of meditation in one sitting.

Nurturing Relationships

There's no doubt that relationships are one of the most important components of our lives. Then why is it that we barely spend a moment thinking about them? Are you taking the time to reflect on how your relationships are going *right now?* Don't wait for signs of trouble before you start paying attention.

Old and New Words of Wisdom

Actions speak louder than words. What do your actions tell your friends? What do their actions tell you?

Recognize that we're all doing the best we can. If there is someone in your family or office with whom you frequently become frustrated, tell yourself the next time you interact with that person that he or she is doing the best he or she can at this moment in life. Notice how that belief eliminates much — if not all — of your frustration with this person.

Make time for people you care about. When was the last time you had a long chat with your best friend? Or hugged your brother or sister? It's so easy to get caught up in doing and achieving that we often neglect to make time to be with the people we care about most.

Keep in touch. Getting an unexpected card or letter in the mail can really brighten up the day for a friend. Buy a bunch of cards or keep a pack of postcards handy to send when the mood strikes. E-mail cards are also a great way to surprise a friend. Check out www.bluemountain.com, where you can select and send an e-mail card for just about any occasion — for free.

Recognize that you cannot change other people. If someone you care about has a problem, don't make it your problem. Just listen and be there.

Give that which you most wish to receive. If you want love and respect, show love and respect. If you want forgiveness, forgive yourself and others.

Be yourself and allow others to be who they are.

Attack the behavior, not the person. If someone's behavior is upsetting to you, make a simple statement such as, "When you [do whatever it is he or she is doing], I feel [whatever it is you are feeling]," and then wait for a response. While the first instinct may be to defend themselves, very often when people learn that their behavior is causing someone undue stress they will want to change that behavior, especially if they value the relationship.

Hold the advice. People often complain about things that are going on in their lives, but they're not necessarily looking for solutions — just an ear. Make it a point to give out advice only when specifically asked.

If you feel you must give unsolicited advice, be gentle. Always include a positive statement with the negative statement. If a friend tries to give you advice you didn't want to hear, try to remember that your friend is doing so because he or she cares about you.

Simple Relationship Practices

Squeeze in friendship moments. If it's hard to make time to go out to dinner or a movie with a friend, try inviting a very close friend to go grocery shopping with you. You can split up once you're in the store. Even a short drive to and from your destination gives you a chance to catch up and feel more a part of each other's lives.

Accept the fact that as you change, your relationships will change. Very often, this change requires a period of adjustment. But not every relationship can withstand change. Some relationships are able to exist only under certain conditions. It's okay to end a friendship that's not working out. If the relationship is not mutually satisfying, it is no longer a friendship.

If you want to get to know someone, ask questions. People like to talk about themselves. Don't you?

Be quick to give thanks. Also, be quick to say "I'm sorry."

Face conflict head-on. Conflict is a normal aspect of everyday life. When you find yourself in a dispute with someone, invite that person to be your ally in finding a solution. Say, "Okay, it appears that we have a conflict. What can we do about it?"

Watch people as well as listening to what they are saying. Nonverbal communication accounts for 93 percent of communication. To hear the whole message, maintain eye contact and observe facial expressions, hand gestures, and body movement.

Listen and learn. When listening, make a conscious effort to let go of memory, desire, and judgment so that for the moments you are listening, you exist only as an ear connected to a heart.

Fostering Love

The love of another is something we all wish to have throughout our lives. A loving relationship makes you feel happy, secure, and content, as well as confident in the feeling that you are worthy of love. But, as we all know, a loving relationship is not easy to maintain, and, in fact, requires a lot of care and work.

Love for Life

Know what you want from a love relationship *before* you enter into one.

An authentic love relationship is a satisfying and fulfilling relationship. It requires that both parties know what they want out of it and communicate this to each other. It is not about one person changing or giving up everything else for the other.

In *Live Your Dream,* author Joyce Chapman suggests that you ask yourself the following questions:

- Does my current relationship support me in living my dream?
- What's working in my relationship?
- Is my partner aware of my needs and desires?
- Are my needs and desires important in our relationship?
- What is the purpose of our relationship?

Surprise your mate every once in a while. Write "I love you" in toothpaste on the mirror, make his or her favorite meal, offer to give a foot massage. Or write a note that expresses your appreciation for a specific personal quality or recent action and pin it to his or her pillow.

Never take any loving relationship for granted. Do, however, allow the relationship to grow and change. Consider yourself and those you love as works in progress.

Create a shared mission statement. Think about what kind of partners you want to be. How do you want to treat each other? Write a succinct statement that sums up your answers in one or two short sentences. For example: "Our mission is to support each other as we strive to achieve our individual dreams. We do this because we believe that it will bring us closer together in body, mind, and spirit."

Actively work at your relationship. Being happy in any relationship takes time, energy, thoughtfulness, and persistence. Invest as much as you would like to receive in return.

Be assertive about your wants and needs. If you are waiting for a loved one to figure out what you might like, be prepared to wait a very long time. No one knows what you want unless you ask for it. Keep requests simple and straightforward and include a time frame, if possible. For example, "Could you please call me as soon as you know that you are going to be running late?" If necessary, rehearse your request until you can ask for what you want without anger, criticism, or whining.

Make and keep a regular weekly date. Set aside time for just the two of you — without distractions like the telephone, pager, and television, and without the kids. Go to your favorite restaurant. Take a walk or a hike. Go to an outdoor concert or festival. Make it a date that lets you connect on as many levels as possible: physically, socially, intellectually, spiritually, emotionally, romantically.

Enjoy simple pleasures together. Entice your partner outside in the evening. Sit side-by-side on the porch steps and listen to crickets, watch fireflies, or just gaze at the stars.

Get touchy. If a picture paints a thousand words, then a touch speaks volumes about the depth of your affection. Touch can also melt defenses. If you feel a fight coming on, reach out and touch your significant other. Face each other and hold both hands as you express feelings of hurt or anger.

Actively listen! Make the effort to listen to — and the extra effort to remember — what your mate tells you about his or her day-to-day life, hopes, and dreams. It's well worth the effort.

Get away. Rekindle passion with a change of scenery. Book a room at a romantic inn or a nice hotel near home. Let your spouse in on the plan — or make it a surprise!

Caring for Family

Family relationships, like love relationships, need a great deal of attention to keep everyone happy. Sometimes this attention might take the form of a specific action, such as a group vacation or outing, while at other times all you need to do is evaluate how your family relationships are doing. Be mindful of yourself and the rest of your family, and you will be able to fully enjoy the good times as well as help each other through the bad times.

How to Be in a "Family Way"

Leave stress at work. Studies have shown that if Mom or Dad comes home grumpy from work, the stress and negative emotions can infect the whole family like chicken pox. If you've had a bad day, do something on the way home to improve your mood. Listen to soothing music in your car or take a brisk walk.

Plan one-on-one time with your children. Try asking children to take turns helping you to prepare dinner. They might balk at first, but will soon begin to look forward to their turn if, during your time together, you shower them with attention. Ask about school, extracurricular activities, friends, favorite subjects, and dreams.

Appreciate your children for who they are — not what you want them to be.

Are You a Good Parent?

You might wish sometimes that you had more time or energy to give your children. And from time to time, you might want to kick yourself for something you said or did. But if your children feel safe, wanted, and loved, that's what really matters.

Fathers: Be mindful. According to a research study at Oxford University in England, fathers who spend as little as five minutes a day talking with their sons help to boost their self-esteem and self-confidence. Talk about their problems, their schoolwork, and their social lives. Do the same for your daughters.

Plan weekly family time. Schedule at least one morning, afternoon, evening, or day every week that provides an opportunity for all family members to have fun together. Take turns making suggestions about what to do next.

Don't blame work if you're unhappy. Studies have shown that men and women alike attribute their emotional state (whether they're happy or depressed) to relationships within the family. If you are unhappy, look at your relationship to the rest of your family. What isn't working for you? What is within your power to change? Express your feelings in a nonaggressive way with a statement that focuses on those feelings. Example: "I feel that you don't appreciate the time I spend cooking meals" versus "You never thank me for making a nice dinner."

Mindfulness in the 21st Century

With every advance in science, medicine, and technology, the pace and complexity of our lives increase. Long ago, for example, when the only way to send a message from one village to another was to send a messenger, messages were fewer and farther between and when they arrived it was a major event. Today, we are bombarded with voice mail, e-mail, and media messages, and it has become increasingly difficult to wade through the clutter to determine what's really important.

What does this mean? Technology has changed the way we live, work, interact, and even think. With laptop computers, for example, we have a harder time separating work from home — even while on vacation. But just as technology has brought people the ability to remain in constant touch, it has also pushed us farther apart. Messages we might have communicated in person or on the telephone we now send via the faceless, voiceless medium of e-mail. We make friends and even look for dates in chat rooms on the Internet. And our reactions to (even thoughts about) current events are shaped by the media, as news is packaged and delivered in the most sensational way.

Following are some tips to help you make conscious choices about the impact of technology on your life and your environment. Remember that there are no right or wrong choices — only what's right or wrong for you.

How Much Stuff Do You Need?

Make conscious choices about gadgets. Take a look at the number of gadgets and appliances in your kitchen — everything from electric can openers to microwaves. Think about the pros and cons of each and then determine if you really need those items. For example, an electric mixer may be easier to use than a wooden spoon, but the spoon is easier to wash. An electric can opener is certainly a convenience, but no use whatsoever in the event of a power outage.

Conduct an experiment with your television. Put your television in a storage closet or unplug it for one full week. At the end of the week, assess the impact of television on your life. What did you miss? What did you do with the time you would have spent watching television?

Turn off the ringer on your telephone. The telephone is a wonderful invention, but unplanned phone calls can be disruptive. When you don't wish to be interrupted, let voice mail or your answering machine answer calls, and call back at a time when you can give your full attention to the caller.

Don't throw out outdated computer equipment; donate it. There are computer-recycling centers springing up all over the country. They will take an old computer or printer, check it to see what still works, and swap in parts from other computers to make it operational. Then they pass the recycled system on to a school, community center, or nonprofit organization.

Buy ink in bulk. If you have a printer that uses ink cartridges, consider buying ink in bulk and refilling cartridges. It keeps a lot of packaging out of our landfills and saves 80 to 90 percent of the cost of packaged cartridges. ACSI Bulk Inks is a reputable source; call (770) 925-2616 or visit its Web site at www.oddparts.com/ink/inkjet.htm.

Recycle toner cartridges. Many laser printer manufacturers have toner-recycling programs. Hewlett-Packard, for example, has a program called HP Planet Partners. Each HP toner cartridge comes with a prepaid UPS return shipping label, so that you can return spent cartridges to the manufacturer.

Steer clear of chatty drivers. Studies have shown that drivers are four to five times more likely to crash while using cellular phones because they are distracted. Here's a sobering fact: If you chat while you drive, the chances of having an accident are about the same as if you were drunk. If you must make a call from your car, pull over.

Schedule an "electronic blackout." For a peaceful evening, unplug the television, turn off the cellular phone, pager, computer, and fax machine, and turn down the volume on the answering machine.

Does having a cell phone simplify or complicate your life? For working people who are frequently away from their desks, a cell phone easily pays for itself in accessibility and time saved. What benefit do you derive from having a cell phone? What's the downside? Can you justify your bill? If you own your own cell phone, you may be able to cancel your contract but still continue using it for 911 calls. Check with your service provider.

ON-LINE OR ON A CRASH COURSE?

It's so easy to surf the Web that some people are finding it hard to stop. Are you addicted to the Internet? Symptoms include:

- An inability to resist going on-line
- Using the Internet to escape problems or improve a bad mood
- Lying about how much time is spent on-line
- Feeling anxious or restless when not using the Internet

Internet Addiction Disorder (IAD) can have serious consequences, including neglect of family, job, or school and a disrupted home life. For more information and resources, check out netaddiction.com or virtual-addiction.com.

Gain Financial Freedom

In this chapter . . .

- *Budgeting and Spending*
- *Reduce Your Debt*
- *Savings and Investments*
- *Living on Less*
- *Creative Frugality*
- *Frugal Family Fun*
- *Frugal Grown-up Fun*

Money may well be at the heart of your cluttered life. Gaining control of your finances is the first step to financial freedom. You may never achieve financial independence, but you can take steps to reduce your debt (and spending) and increase your savings and investments so that you don't have to worry so much about money. *That's* financial freedom.

What are your beliefs about money? Is money an end in itself or a means to something? How much is enough? Many people are discovering that less is more. The less you spend, the less you need to work. And the less you have to work, the more time you have for the things that really matter.

Budgeting and Spending

The best way to figure out where your money goes is to keep track of every penny you spend for an entire month. It's helpful if you use a form like the one on pages 94 and 95. Fill out a form each week for one month and then total what you spent in each category. Once you know where all your money is going, you can develop a realistic budget that is much easier to maintain.

Making Budgets Work

Resist the urge to have immediate gratification. Change your mind-set from "I want it now" to "If I wait, there's something better I can have later."

Stick to your budget. Once you have established a realistic budget, make a conscientious effort to stick to it for at least three months. At the end of each month, compare your budget figures to actual figures. If you are way off course after the first month, see if you can make a couple of adjustments during the next month to bring those numbers closer together. After a few months, you should need to make only minor adjustments.

Shopping for a car? Consider buying a good used car instead of a new car. Use the money you save by having a lower car payment to reduce your debt, or put the money toward savings and investments each month.

WHERE DOES ALL YOUR MONEY GO?

EXPENSE	DAY 1	DAY 2	DAY 3
Gasoline			
Eating Out			
Entertainment			
Food at Work			
Groceries			
Clothing			
Gifts/Cards			
Dry Cleaning			
Personal Items			
Magazines/Newspapers			
Car Payment			
Mortgage Payment			
Credit Card Payment			
Loan Payment			
Other			
Total			

Try the cash system for nonbill expenses. Create separate envelopes for groceries, gas, entertainment, and other regularly occurring expenses. Each week, put into these envelopes the cash amount you have budgeted for each expense. Borrow cash from another expense envelope only if you are absolutely sure that you will not need it for that expense.

Day 4	Day 5	Day 6	Day 7	Total

Are you paying too much for your own money? Automatic teller machines (ATMs) are a wonderfully convenient way to access your money, but ATM fees can add up. Make it a point to find and use ATMs that do not charge you for your own money. Or if you have been going to the ATM three times a week, take out your usual weekly withdrawal once a week or even biweekly so you have one fee instead of three or more.

Make a few little cutbacks. Look at your spending over the past week. Where might you be able to cut back on spending without affecting the quality of your life? Many people spend $5 a day or more on lunches. That's $1,300 a year! You could save money by bringing your lunch from home.

Look for "cash cushions." Money above and beyond the amount needed to pay monthly bills and expenses often gets frittered away. Use it toward debt reduction or savings.

Save before you spend. Arrange for automatic transfers from your paycheck to an investment or savings account. Doing this will give you more security and, ultimately, financial freedom.

Know the difference between wants and needs. We *need* food, water, shelter, and clothing. We *want* gourmet meals, big-screen televisions, fancy cars, and stylish apparel. Before you go shopping for a particular item, ask yourself whether it is something you need or something you want. If it's luxury item and you really "must" have it, develop a budget for it.

No-Fuss Bill Paying

Use the list method. Another way to manage payments is to put all unpaid bills in a "To Be Paid" folder with a list of each bill, the amount due, and

Let Your Credit Cards Pay You

If credit cards are a necessity, choose cards that pay you to use them. Credit cards like the Discover Card offer cash back on total annual purchases. If you use it for everything (groceries, gas, restaurants, travel, and so on), you get back a little something every year to add to your savings or investment fund. The key is to pay off your balance every month; otherwise the interest you pay will far outweigh the cash you get back. And be sure to choose a card that does not charge an annual fee.

the due date. As you pay each bill, cross it off the list. Add new bills to the bottom of the list. Write check numbers on paid bills and file in folders designated for each specific category: for example, telephone, car insurance.

Pay bills twice a month. Use a folder with two pockets — one for bills to be paid on the first of the month and one for bills to be paid on the fifteenth. Keep this folder handy so that you can put bills into the appropriate pocket when they arrive.

Fill a three-ring binder with pocket folders for filing receipts and bills by category. You can easily keep track of payments by writing the check number, amount, and date paid on each folder. This method is especially handy if you have a lot of household expenses that are tax deductible, because you'll have everything in one place when tax time rolls around. And it eliminates filing monthly bills.

Spend Wisely

Look at the real cost of your purchases. Think in terms of how many hours you need to work to pay for each item you want to buy. For example, if you earn $15 an hour and an item costs $120, ask yourself if you would be willing to work eight hours to have that item.

Trade credit cards for debit cards. A debit card combines the convenience of a credit card with the sensibility of paying cash. Debit cards are different from credit cards, as they are tied to cash in a bank account. They are particularly useful for making airline, hotel, or car rental reservations over the telephone.

Use only cash when shopping. When you shop with cash, you put more thought into each purchase. And you don't have to spend any time wondering if you can really afford something: Either you have enough cash or you don't.

Reduce Your Debt

You don't need to make more money to reduce your debt. You simply need to change what you do with the money you have. Keep reading.

Getting Out of Credit Card Debt

Take a good look at your credit card statements. About 30 to 40 percent of your minimum monthly payment goes toward interest and only 60 to 70 percent goes toward reducing your actual debt. So if your minimum monthly payment is $50, you're paying $15 to $20 every month for nothing. Even if you don't charge another thing on your credit cards, it can take a surprising number of years to pay off what you owe when you pay only the minimum amount due each month. Here's a foolproof plan for getting rid of credit card debt.

1. List your debts in order of the lowest to highest amounts owed. Use whatever money you have freed up in your budgeting process to pay extra toward the first debt on your list.
2. Pay the minimum amount due on the other debts. Continue to do this each month until the first debt on your list is paid. Here's where you really start making progress.
3. Combine the amount you've been paying on the first debt to the minimum monthly amount due on the next debt until it too is paid. Continue this process until all debt is paid.
4. Begin to apply your total debt reduction payment each month to savings and investments.

Make payments on time every month. If you make even one late payment or skip a payment one month, many credit card companies will increase your interest rate dramatically. So it will take even longer to pay off your debt. If you must, make a late payment to a more lenient creditor such as the telephone or electric company.

Use bankruptcy as a last resort. Filing for bankruptcy may seem like an easy out, but a bankruptcy remains on your credit report for 10 years and will affect your ability to secure a loan for a car or home. It also may rear its ugly head in a routine employment check and cost you a job.

Pay attention to notices on your bill. Some credit companies will try to raise your interest rate for no reason at all. But they are required by law to notify you in advance and give you the option of declining the higher rate of interest. This generally requires writing a letter to the address they provide. Do it.

Pare down to one credit card. Reducing the number of credit cards you have can cut your debt and simplify your life with fewer bills to pay.

Avoid debt traps. If you are paying on a credit card or loan, you may receive credit checks from time to time with an enticement to use them to go on a well-deserved vacation, install a backyard pool for some summertime fun, or simply give yourself a nice cash bonus. Don't do it; it's a debt trap. Rip up the checks (so no one else can use them) and throw them away immediately.

Don't try ducking creditors. You'll actually buy yourself more time if you settle on an amount and show that you are willing to repay your debt. If you are having difficulty making minimum monthly payments, contact the Consumer Credit Counseling Service in your area (check your Yellow Pages or call toll-free information).

Freeze your credit — literally. If you tend to overspend on credit, put your credit cards in a small plastic tub filled with water and place the tub in the freezer. Freezing your credit cards will curb impulse credit card shopping by helping you make a conscious choice about what and when you will buy on credit. Once you get used to buying with cash (and you see your credit card balances going down), you may want to thaw and then cut up those credit cards.

Close unused credit accounts. It's a good idea to cancel credit cards that are paid in full for two reasons. First, it will keep you from getting sucked back into charging. Second, the credit card companies will notify the credit reporting agencies and your credit file will be updated. This is important because having too much open credit could result in a loan denial for a major purchase such as a home or car.

Don't use credit to pay back credit. If you're short one month, you may be tempted to take a cash advance on one credit card to pay the monthly

---

WHAT IS THE REAL COST OF DEBT?

There's a great on-line publication called *bankrate.com* that is an excellent source of articles and information to help you manage your credit. The Web site includes a debt repayment calculator that figures the real cost of your debt: that is, how much you end up paying in interest.

Go to www.bankrate.com and click on "Credit Cards." Then click on "Cost of Debt" to bring up the calculator. Enter the total balance of each credit card or loan and the rate of interest you pay for each. Then enter the number of years in which you want to pay off the balance. This will give you the amount you need to pay each month to achieve your goal. The calculator also lets you compare the total interest you pay — or the real cost of your debt — based on the length of the loan.

payment due on another card. Don't do it! You're just digging yourself deeper into debt.

Don't blow a windfall. If you receive a tax refund or any other significant sum of cash, resist the urge to spend it. Apply the whole thing toward a debt and you'll be free that much sooner from monthly payments.

Savings and Investments

If you've got a steady job, chances are very good that you're spending money as fast as you earn it, and that you have a hard time keeping yourself from dipping into your savings for this and that. You might not be worried now about what you're going to live on when you retire, but the sooner you start putting money away, the more money you'll have when the time comes. Here are a few ideas to get you started.

Build for the Future

Make your money work harder. Consider moving money from traditional savings and money market accounts to certificates of deposit. A certificate of deposit allows you to deposit a certain amount of money as an investment for a fixed length of time, ranging from three months to five years. CDs are federally insured and pay much higher rates of return.

Pay yourself first. Before you start writing out checks for bills, make a payment to a savings or investment account. Make it a habit to save something each month — even if it's only $10. Increase that amount as you pay off debts or get pay raises.

Live within your means by using the 70-20-10 rule. Use 70 percent of your take-home pay for regular monthly bills plus other regular expenses such as groceries, gas, and clothing. Set aside 20 percent for large-ticket items such as a car or home. Save the remaining 10 percent. This will help keep you from overextending yourself with credit.

Spend less, invest more. Use automatic payments from your paycheck (or checking or savings account) to fund investment contributions and learn to live on what's left rather than overspending and finding yourself unable to make regular contributions.

Contribute annually to an IRA. The government allows a tax deduction of up to $2,000 a year ($4,000 if you file jointly) when you invest in a regular Individual Retirement Account (IRA). Your investment will grow tax-deferred until you begin to withdraw at retirement. Check with your tax specialist for options, restrictions, and eligibility requirements.

Fund your 401K to the max. If your company offers a 401K program, take full advantage of it. Automatic deductions from your paycheck make it a painless way to save for retirement. Some companies even offer to match part of your contribution, which really helps your balance grow.

Invest all extra income. Whether you get a nice tax refund or raise or win the lottery, plan to invest any extra cash that comes your way rather than spend it.

Use CDs to save for large expenditures. Plan ahead and sock away money for vacation or holidays.

Involve the whole family in saving. Ask family members to think of ways they can save money each week. Keep a chart of the money saved so that you can monitor your progress. Offer a reward such as a family trip for reaching the goal.

Look at the little picture. Let's say, for example, that you want to save $2,000 over the next year. That works out to $5.48 a day. Now look at your daily expenses. Where might you be able to cut back by $5.48 each day? Start putting away that amount — in cash — every day. At the end of the week, take your saved money to the bank and deposit it your savings account.

Save your loose change. Get into the habit — and encourage family members to get in the habit — of putting all loose change in a jar every night. At the end of the week, roll up your change and deposit it in your savings account.

Living on Less

If you are struggling to make ends meet, you can reclaim control over your finances — and your life — by choosing to consume less. Consuming less also saves trees, mineral resources, water, and the environment.

Reducing Food Costs

Take out instead of eating out. When you eat out, you have to add an extra 15 to 20 percent to the bill for service and you pay a ridiculous price for beverages. Ordering takeout allows you to save on the "added costs" of eating out while enjoying the same quality of food.

Eat out less. If you eat out once a week, make it once a month. Too tired to cook at night? Cook large meals on the weekends and eat leftovers during the week. And use your slow cooker! Prepare ingredients the night before and throw them into the pot before leaving for work. Coming home to a hot meal is like having a cook. And you have only one pot to wash.

Plan ahead and save on lunch costs. Make up a week's worth of sandwiches on the weekend and freeze them in separate plastic bags, then place them all in a large airtight bag. Remove sandwiches from the freezer each morning and they will be defrosted by lunchtime. Fillings that freeze well include peanut butter, ham, bologna, salami, turkey, chicken, pastrami, roast beef or pork, and tuna made with sour cream or salad dressing. Mayonnaise, cheese, and jelly do not freeze well.

Buy food in bulk. Stock up on canned goods when they go on sale. Buy large bags of flour, sugar, rice, pasta, and beans from your local food cooperative or wholesale club. Not enough storage space in your kitchen? Store it in your basement or garage (providing they are dry), out of the reach of potential pests. Make room in a linen closet, bathroom cupboard, or hallway closet. Or store extra supplies under your bed in labeled boxes, with labels facing out.

Eat out earlier in the day. If you enjoy going out to eat but don't enjoy paying the high price of a gourmet dinner, go out for a gourmet brunch or lunch instead for about half the price — or less.

Grow a vegetable garden. Plan meals around what's in season. Trade produce with neighbors and coworkers.

Eat vegetarian more often. Eating meat less often will reduce your food bill considerably. Substitute main dishes that feature eggs, beans, cheese, or tofu as a source of protein.

Saving — Simply

Take care of what you own. When you buy items, choose high quality over low price. High-quality, high-efficiency, durable goods will last longer and can be repaired if necessary.

Buy only out of need, such as to replace something that is used up, worn out, or broken beyond repair.

Donate clothes to charity and deduct the expense from your income taxes. For every $100 worth of clothing you donate, you could save yourself 15 to 33 percent in taxes at the end of the year. Just be sure to keep a list of the items you donate, along with the value of each item, and ask for a tax-deductible receipt from the charity to which you donate. *Note:* This works only if you itemize your taxes.

Learn to want what you have. Look at the many things you own. Do you wear all of your jewelry and clothes? Probably not. Do you use all the gadgets in your kitchen? Probably not. Do you have more material possessions than your parents and grandparents did? Probably. Be thankful for the abundance in your life.

Get cash for clothes you aren't wearing by selling them on consignment. Clothes must be in excellent condition and relatively new or classically styled. Typically, there is a 60- to 90-day contract period in which your clothes will be for sale in the shop, and the seller (that's you) gets 40 to 50 percent of the selling price. *Bonus tip:* Make even more money by picking up good, cheap clothes at yard sales and then selling them on consignment.

Get rid of a car. If you have one car that is not driven every day, compare the cost of owning a car with the cost of renting a car or taking a cab on the occasions when you need a vehicle.

STOP JUNK MAIL!

How often do you get offers in the mail that happen to be something you were looking for? More often than not, it's seeing a product or offer that makes us think we want it. To stop junk mail, write to:

> Mail Preference Service
> Direct Marketing Association
> P.O. Box 9008
> Farmingdale, NY 11735-9008

Allow several months for the deluge to subside. Meanwhile, make a commitment to throw out every catalog and direct-mail offer without even opening it.

Save on holiday gifts and seasonal items. Buy greeting cards, wrapping paper, and seasonal decorations at half price right after the holidays. For very inexpensive gifts, look for almost-new items at garage sales, secondhand stores, consignment shops, and thrift shops. Or start early and make your own gifts.

Avoid impulse buying. Shop with a list and stick to what's on your list. If you see something else you want, resist the urge to buy it on the spot. Go home and think about it for a few days and then decide if it's worth going back for.

Tune out commercial messages. Advertising creates desire. Use commercial breaks to get up and stretch, do a couple of quick household chores, or simply turn down the volume and talk to other members in your household.

> *To live content within small means: to seek elegance rather than luxury and refinement rather than fashion; to be worthy, not respectable, and wealthy, not rich; to listen to stars and birds, to babies and sages with open heart; in a word, to let the spiritual unbidden and unconscious grow up through the common.*
>
> — Ralph Waldo Emerson

Learn to do it yourself. If you can do some of your own repairs or make things you might normally buy, you can save quite a lot of money. See if you can find someone who is willing to teach you what you need to learn. Your local high school or community college may offer continuing education classes. Or teach yourself using books from the library.

Rent videos instead of going to the movies. Save even more by choosing movies that have been out for a while rather than new releases.

Cash In on Specials

Take advantage of membership discounts. Many organizations and associations frequently offer member discounts on a variety of products and services, but most people don't use them because they forget that they are available. Write down on a slip of paper all of the discounts available to you and then carry it in your wallet or purse as a reminder.

Take advantage of off-peak discounts. Some museums offer free admission on certain days of the week. Attend a movie matinee instead of a prime-time show and save some cash. Look for restaurants that offer early-bird dinner specials (usually between 4 P.M. and 6 P.M.). Attend plays on weeknights instead of weekends or go to a preview performance.

Buy movie tickets in bulk. Many movie theater chains offer tickets by mail, which allows you to save about 40 percent off the regular price. Ask your local theater.

Creative Frugality

Are you aware of all the free and reduced-cost activities and items available to you? There are numerous opportunities out there — if you know where to look. All it takes is a little creative thinking, and the desire to have fun for free!

Trade baby-sitting services. If you and your significant other would like to have the house to yourselves for the night (a priceless treat!), make arrangements ahead of time to have your children spend the night with friends or family members, with the understanding that you will take in their children another night.

If you can't beat 'em, join 'em. Kids love fast food, but even fast food can get expensive. Why not try re-creating your kids' favorite fast food entrée at home? Betsy Sullivan, editor of *Balancing Act,* a frugality newsletter, tells the story of how she and her boys succeeded in creating a chicken fajita that tasted very much like the one served at McDonald's. They bought one chicken fajita, took it home, pulled it apart, and figured out how to make it. And they had a great time doing it!

Decorate for free. Some local libraries loan out framed paintings and other works of art. All you need is a valid library card and you can bring home a "new" painting or two every month. Seashells, unusual rocks, pinecones, and other natural artifacts can be displayed in canning jars and baskets or made into an artistic arrangement. And, of course, there's nothing like a bouquet of wildflowers to brighten a room.

See plays and concerts for free. Many theaters and concert halls recruit volunteer ushers, who get to enjoy the performance once everyone is seated. Volunteers may even get to meet the performers!

Vacation at home. It's simpler, less expensive, and can be far more relaxing than jetting (or driving) to and from a vacation destination. Create an itinerary just as you would for a regular vacation. Plan to see the local sights that visitors come to see. Try out a new restaurant or two. Order takeout or have food delivered on other nights. Stock up on your favorite breakfast foods, snacks, and beverages. Unplug the telephone, television, and computer. Leave housework for when you "get back." You're on vacation!

Frugal Family Fun

Extend your creative frugality into activities for the whole family. There is so much no- and low-cost entertainment, if you know where to look.

Let the Good Times Roll

You don't have to spend a lot of money for kids to have fun. Check your local newspaper for upcoming events and activities — free festivals, fairs, and other forms of entertainment — that offer frugal fun for the whole family.

Let your kids camp out in the backyard for memories that will last a lifetime.

GREAT FAMILY FUN IDEAS ON-LINE

Whether you're looking for indoor or outdoor activities, arts and crafts ideas, or fun learning activities, you'll find hundreds of tips and ideas on-line. Go to www.momsonline.com and click on "Hot Tips." At this Web site, you'll also find general money-saving tips, plus lots of valuable information for parents.

For fun learning activities, check out the Family Education Network at www.familyedu-cation.com. Select an age group and then click on an activity topic. You also can sign up for a free e-mail newsletter.

Another Web site that lets you select activities by age group is ParentTime, which can be found at www.pathfinder.com/parenttime. At Parent Soup (www.parentsoup.com), click on "Education Central" and then "Fun Learning."

Plant a vegetable garden. Kids love to watch things grow, especially if they have a hand in planting and caring for them. Bonus: Once those veggies are ready to pick, you save on produce!

Bring your own. If you plan a trip to an amusement park or other venue that charges exorbitant prices for food and beverages, don't blow your hard-earned money on expensive drinks and snacks. Load a child's wagon with a small cooler and tow it along with you. If there's enough room, young children can ride in the wagon when they get tired.

Take a walk — and talk. Sure, the exercise will do you all good, but the most important benefit of this activity is that it allows you to give your kids what they crave more than anything — your attention. Let them talk about whatever is on their minds.

Take a camping trip. Hotel stays and eating out make up the bulk of expenses on vacation. Camping and cookouts minimize those expenses plus add fun and adventure to your trip.

Allow kids to become bored. When kids get bored, their imaginations kick in and they come up with truly creative ways to entertain themselves. It's a wonderful way to help children develop and enhance creativity, imagination, and resourcefulness.

Enjoy simple pleasures as a family. Chances are good that the pace of life for your kids is far more hectic than it was for you when you were their age. Following are some ideas for slowing down the pace with some simple, old-fashioned fun:

- Pick your own apples or berries.
- Bake cookies or cupcakes.
- Play board games.
- Go fly a kite.
- Build a fort — indoors or outdoors.
- Have a neighborhood sidewalk drawing contest.
- Take a family bike ride.
- Bring a picnic lunch to the beach.
- Rent a rowboat on a nearby lake.
- Schedule a family reading hour.
- Put on a play or skit.

See what's happening at bookstores. Like libraries, many bookstores offer a variety of free activities for children, including:

- Children's video release parties
- Storytelling times
- Young readers' clubs

Visit your library. Many libraries offer a variety of free activities for children of all ages, including:

- Weekly storytelling hours for children
- Summer reading clubs for children
- Writing workshops

Frugal Grown-up Fun

Sure, kids are easily amused, but that doesn't mean there isn't a variety of low-cost activities for you "big kids" too. Scan local newspapers, as well as ads and brochures on community bulletin boards, to find out what's happening in your area.

Plan a picnic. Pack a basket, knapsack, or cooler with the makings of a gourmet brunch, lunch, or dinner — complete with the beverages of your choice. Don't forget to bring along a blanket or cloth to spread on the ground.

Give yourself a visitor's tour. Go to your nearest visitors center and pick up some local-interest brochures or ask about fun things to do. Choose places and activities that are new to you.

INTERNET TRAVEL BARGAINS

Go to www.smarterliving.com to sign up for free e-mail newsletters that alert you to deals on airfares, hotels, and car rentals as well as last-minute travel deals from the cities you preselect. When you sign up for the free newsletters, you automatically become a member, which entitles you to discounts on car rentals. The Web site also includes links to other useful sites for requesting visitor guides, weather reports, and maps of your destination.

Throw potluck dinner parties. If you enjoy entertaining but want to keep the cost down, invite friends to a potluck dinner party. Ask them to bring their favorite dish. You can request specific courses or just see what kind of dinner develops!

Visit your local library. Larger public libraries offer a variety of programs and services that are free and open to the public, including:

- Free Internet access
- Writing workshops
- How-to demonstrations and mini seminars
- Book and poetry readings
- Book discussion groups
- Current magazines and newspapers
- Special-interest exhibits
- Free video- and audiocassette loans

Check out what's happening at bookstores. Many bookstores, especially those with cafés, offer a regular schedule of events and activities, including:

- Book and poetry readings
- Writers groups
- Book discussion groups
- Free live music
- Special-interest discussions

Step 6

Lighten Your Load

In this chapter . . .

- *Unclutter Your Home*
- *Minimize Stress*
- *Let It Go*
- *Lighten Up!*
- *Free Up Time*

Into each life, a little clutter must fall. But that doesn't mean you have to hold on to it forever! If your life feels out of balance, you might want to lighten your load; that is, free up time, space, and energy for more important things.

Start by paring down your material possessions to those things you either love or use regularly. Lighten your mind by learning to minimize stress. Lighten your heart by letting go of guilt, anger, and other negative emotions and adding more humor and laughter. You'll be healthier and happier for it.

Unclutter Your Home

How much is enough? Do you really need 23 pairs of shoes? Or seven sets of sheets for your bed? Or that handy-dandy gadget you just saw advertised on television? How many things that you have bought are still in your home but not being used?

Acquiring things has become such a habit that we often don't consider the cost of acquisition. Think about the price you pay — not just the cost of purchasing, but also the cost of owning. Material possessions cost you storage space and they cost you the time it takes to shop and care for them. The more you own, the more you have to care for.

No matter how much you acquire, you will never have it all. Better to have a few possessions that you love and use than a thousand that weigh you down.

Get Back to Basics

There's no right way to unclutter your home and no one way that works for everyone. What's important to remember is that *getting* started is far more important than *how* you get started!

Do not try to unclutter your whole house at once. Work in one room at a time and don't switch to another room until you're done. Seeing progress will motivate you to keep up the good work.

Clean out one drawer each night. You will make progress toward your goal each day and it won't seem like such a huge project.

Plan uncluttering activities around garbage days or plan to take stuff to the dump or your selected charity that day. Otherwise, you may be tempted to reconsider.

Start with the easy stuff. This will get you into the act of uncluttering with little or no pain or anxiety. Get a large garbage bag and walk through your house. Throw out anything that is clearly garbage:

- Expired medicines
- Expired coupons
- Outdated clothes
- Makeup that's more than one year old
- Sunscreen that's more than two years old
- Things that are broken (unless they are valuable and fixable)
- Odd socks
- Grocery bags (10 is enough!)
- Old restaurant and shopping guides
- Outdated calendars
- Spoiled food
- Rusted utensils and tools
- Travel literature and maps (unless they are new and you have definite plans to travel in the next three months)

Sort belongings into three categories: what you definitely use, what you definitely don't use, and things you can't separate into either of those categories. Put away the things you use. Give away the things you don't use. Store in boxes those things you probably don't use but can't part with just yet. If in six months you haven't opened your boxes, give the items away.

Start with a single drawer. Empty the contents, so you can see everything. Pick up each item and make a decision. If you haven't used or needed that item in the last year or simply don't like or want it anymore, put it in a trash bag. Organize what's left by putting like things together in a box or using rubber bands or plastic bags to contain them.

DETERMINING WHAT TO KEEP

As you decide the relative merit of each item, ask yourself the following questions:

- When was the last time I used this?
- Why don't I use it more often?
- Does it have any sentimental value?
- Do I love it?
- What is the worst possible thing that could happen if I just threw it away? Can I live with that?
- Could I get another one if I needed to?
- If I keep it, where should it go?
- How many of these do I need?

Where to Put It

Designate one room or space for all papers. This is where you pay bills and file them. That way, when you're looking for a particular piece of paperwork, you have automatically narrowed your search.

Look for hiding places — for your clutter, not you! Store extra table leaves under your sofa and linens in boxes under your bed. Use decorative screens and curtains to hide cluttered areas.

Store things where you use them. For instance, if you keep your bathroom cleaning supplies under the bathroom sink, it makes it easy to tackle the job at any time and eliminates unnecessary steps. Rearrange kitchen cabinets so that glasses and plates are near the dishwasher.

Minimize Stress

It would be difficult to discuss the topic of uncluttering your life without bringing up the "S" word. No, the other one: stress.

You might think that eliminating all stress from your life is the answer, but stress isn't the problem. There are two types of stress: eustress, which is positive, and distress, which is negative. Eustress is good because it helps motivate us and enhance our performance. But too much eustress, such as having to cope with one mental or physical challenge after another, can quickly lead to distress.

We can't prevent stress altogether, but we do have a choice about how we react to stress. Of course, our first choice may be to "fight or take flight," which is natural. But with practice, we can moderate or change our reaction to stress so that once-tense situations are far less stressful or no longer stressful at all.

TOP 10 STRESSORS

If you experience one or more of the following at one time or in close succession, you can expect to experience stress.

1. Death of a spouse
2. Divorce
3. Marital separation
4. Jail term
5. Death of a close family member
6. Personal injury or illness
7. Marriage
8. Being fired from your job
9. Marital reconciliation
10. Retirement

Coping Mentally

Keep expectations reasonable. Why set yourself up for failure? You can't please everyone; the sooner you accept that, the sooner you'll begin to feel less frustrated.

Know your body's stress signals. Recognize the emotional and physical clues that plague you when under stress: tight upper back, diarrhea or heartburn, craving for carbohydrates, skin problems, forgetfulness, mental fuzziness, bumping into things. When you get the distress signal — whatever it is — don't ignore it.

Take charge. Think about what specifically is bothering you, such as an upcoming event, family problem, or potential layoff at work. Is there something you can do about it? Identify some possible solutions. Then work on a plan. Get whatever help you need from your partner, a friend, or a professional and then take action.

Inject some humor into your situation. You may not be able to control what is causing you stress, but you can change your reaction to it. Look for whatever humor may be present. Has a "comedy of errors" led you to your present circumstances? Imagine that you are a stand-up comedian explaining your situation or predicament.

Create a sacred place. This can be as simple as a corner of your bedroom with a throw pillow and candle on the floor or as elaborate as a room or an entire house designed using the principles of feng shui. What you want to create is a quiet, peaceful place in which you can close your eyes and shut out the noise and "busyness" of the world around you.

Laugh a little more. Laughter will help you relax — physically and psychologically. Make it a point to spend time with people who make you laugh. When choosing which movies or videos to see, choose comedies over tragedies. Read the comic strips in your daily newspaper.

Hold on to family ties and friendships. Research shows that people who have family and friends to help them through stressful times stay healthier and recover faster than those who do not have a social support system.

Seek help. If stress is affecting your ability to engage in your regular routine (eating, sleeping, working), don't hesitate to talk to a trusted friend or professional counselor.

Slow down. Focus on the quality of your life instead of on getting ahead.

Find a creative outlet. Draw or paint. Make a birthday card with pictures and letters cut out of magazines. Grow a garden. Write a poem or a letter.

Coping Physically

Cultivate healthy habits *before* you feel stressed. Quit smoking. Exercise regularly. Limit consumption of alcohol. Eat a balanced diet that's rich in fruits and vegetables. These simple practices will help your body cope with the physical changes brought on by stress.

Eat well. Good nutrition provides your body with energy stores to draw upon during stressful times. Eating well also makes you feel more in control and better about yourself.

Exercise. Why is it that whatever the question, exercise is the answer? Try it and see. Regular exercise is one of the ultimate stress-beaters. It not only eases mild depression and anxiety, it also makes you feel better about your body, which makes you feel better about yourself. But don't overdo it. Not getting enough rest after workouts can backfire by creating more stress on the body.

Meditate stress away. Just sit in a chair and close your eyes. Visualize a rope with many knots being lowered slowly into a large body of water and one by one, the knots disappear as you repeat the phrase "Relax . . . let go."

The bigger the stress, the more we have to relax. Develop an arsenal of stress techniques that work for you. Simple breathing techniques, for example, can keep you from blowing your top in a meeting. Vigorous exercise after work can help you let go of the day's frustrations.

Caution! If you are under stress, you are also likely to be distracted. Remind yourself to focus on difficult tasks during stressful times. In particular, drive extra carefully or have someone else drive.

Try yoga. Yoga is the 5,000-year-old remedy for stress. It's an integrated practice of gentle stretching, physical postures, breathing exercises, relaxation techniques, and meditation that can help reduce stress, renew energy, and produce a sense of well-being. It also helps develop strength, flexibility, balance, and coordination. Research has shown that yoga offers beneficial effects for many common ailments, such as repetitive stress injuries, backaches, insomnia, and heart disease.

Get plenty of sleep. Lack of sleep is one of the chief causes of daytime fatigue, which can lead to traffic accidents and on-the-job injuries. Research suggests that sleep deprivation boosts levels of stress-related hormones, like adrenaline, which in turn increases the risk of hypertension, stroke, and other cardiovascular problems. Sleep deficiency is also associated with lowered immunity to illness and disease. Following are some tips for getting a better night's sleep:

- Go to bed at a regular time each night.
- Avoid stimulants like tea, coffee, cola, and cocoa before going to bed.
- Eat dinner three to four hours before going to bed to allow time for your body to digest it.

- Exercise every day, but do it early in the day, rather than later.
- Use your bedroom primarily for sleeping — not for activities like eating, reading, and watching television in bed.
- Set your alarm for the same time every day to establish a regular sleep schedule.
- Avoid or limit daytime naps.
- Listen to relaxation tapes to fall asleep.
- If you can't get to sleep within 15 minutes, get up and read or watch television until you feel sleepy.

ON-LINE HELP FOR STRESS MANAGEMENT

There is a wealth of reliable information on the Internet about all aspects of stress — from what it is to how to manage it in your life. An excellent place to start looking for answers to your questions is Internet Mental Health at www.mentalhealth.com. Also check out the Web site for the International Stress Management Association, which is located at www.stress-management-isma.org.

Let It Go

It makes sense that when we're feeling happy and peaceful, we want to hold on to our happiness or peaceful state forever. But why are we so reluctant to let go of unhappy emotions? Letting go doesn't mean suppressing emotions; that's like putting an adhesive bandage on a serious wound. Sure, you can't see it when you cover it up, but it's still festering underneath the bandage. And it just keeps getting worse. The same is true for emotional wounds. It's important to air negative feelings and mistakes — and then let them go so that you can heal.

Learning How to Release

Close your eyes and imagine that you are riding on the wings of an angel. From this great distance, you see your physical self way down below. You notice that wherever you go, whatever you do, there's a dark cloud directly over your head. The cloud is so full of negative emotions (anger, guilt, or frustration) that they are beginning to rain down on you and that's all you can feel. Something inside (or was it the voice of your angel?) urges you to take a deep breath and blow away that cloud. See the "poof" of your breath as it pushes the dark cloud away. Watch it vanish into thin air and then feel the sunlight begin to warm you from the inside out. Enjoy the light for a few minutes before opening your eyes and rejoining with your loving self.

Identify the fear. Anger is a defense mechanism in response to a perceived danger or threat. When you are angry, ask yourself what you are frightened of. If someone is angry with you, try to figure out what might be frightening that person. The best thing you can do is to show compassion.

Learn your lesson. People often say, "Things happen for a reason." When something upsetting happens, think about why it happened to you and why it happened at this particular time in your life. What have you learned or gained from this experience?

Don't get even; get angry. If you can't express your anger to the party that has angered you, stand in front of a mirror and express it to yourself. Let it all out and then let it go.

Forgive yourself, and forgive others. Take a deep breath and exhale the guilt, anger, and resentment. What's done is done. Is there any way you can make amends? Until you can forgive what happened in the past, you cannot live freely and joyfully in the present. Don't waste another second of precious life imprisoned in the past; forgive and forget, or at least forgive and move on.

Shed some inhibitions. Articulate a "taboo" or fear and then break it. For instance, if you've never gone to the movies alone, try it. If you are afraid of a particular item or activity, read up on the subject and then look for an opportunity to be exposed to your fear — without fearing for your safety. Enlist the aid of a trusted friend or a professional.

> *Forgiving can be the beginning of the healing process. We must remember that hatred is like acid. It does more damage to the vessel in which it is stored than to the object on which it is poured.*
>
> — Ann Landers

Lighten Up!

Many aspects of everyday living are serious, but that doesn't mean you can't look for the humor in life. Allow yourself to enjoy your family, friends, and surroundings, and your life will be all the richer for it.

Guarantee more fun in your life. Put yourself in situations you enjoy and in the company of people you enjoy.

Take time to play. If you're walking past a playground, stop and swing awhile. Or take a trip down the slide.

When in doubt, laugh. Let it out. A good belly laugh not only feels good, but it also gives your abdominal muscles a good workout, along with easing tension and stress.

Learn to roll with the punches. Think of someone you know who always seems to be happy, no matter what happens. There's something he or she is doing that's different from what you are doing in response to life's punches. See if you can figure out what it is. Or ask, "What's your secret?"

Don't take yourself so seriously. Make a funny face in the mirror. Now make a *really* funny face.

Put things into perspective. Rate what happens to you on a scale of one to ten. Not everything is an eight, nine, or ten. Save your energy for the truly big stuff.

Double your happiness: Share it!

Don't Underestimate the Power of Exercise

By now you know all about the physical benefits of exercise. But did you know that you can also improve your mood through exercise? In a six-week study, 85 women completed mood surveys before and after exercise. Working out put them in better humor, say researchers at Concordia University in Montreal.

Spare yourself the clutter caused by bad feelings. Participate in activities that make you feel good; eliminate or reduce your participation in activities that don't.

Change Your Point of View

Go with the flow. Being flexible allows greater enjoyment of today. An appointment that gets canceled, for example, is an opportunity to enjoy some unexpected free time.

Adjust your attitude. When you are faced with one of life's lessons in patience, such as a traffic jam or a long line at the checkout, remember that while you may have no control over the situation, your attitude is always within your control. You can choose to be angry and frustrated, or you can choose to remain calm and relaxed. Strike up a conversation with a total stranger. Or entertain yourself by looking at the people around you and making up stories about their lives.

Sing and dance away negative emotions. In using voice and movement, we free negative energy that is stored within our bodies. Try it next time you are home alone. Put on your favorite music and sing and dance to it. If you've got a good imagination, pretend that you're a famous performer in front of a very receptive audience. Don't forget to take a bow!

State your intention to do better. If it is difficult for you to let go of negative emotions, create an affirmation to help you. Your affirmation might be something like "I am a loving, forgiving person" or "My heart radiates the healing energy of forgiveness." Repeat your affirmation aloud a few times every day.

Free Up Time

Research shows that Americans (with the exception of parents with young children) have about 40 more hours of free time each week than previous generations. According to Geoff Godbey, a professor of leisure studies at Penn State University and coauthor of *Time for Life,* about 25 hours of free time come during weekdays, usually in 30- to 45-minute increments. But the typical American estimates his or her weekly amount of free time at 19 hours. Perhaps that is because we watch an average of 16 to 21 hours of television each week! Just think of what you might be able to do and enjoy with that extra 20 hours or so of free time each week.

Waste Not, Want Not

Harness your energy. Whether it's first thing in the morning or late at night, there's a time of day that is generally your most productive time. Use this time to accomplish those things that require the largest amount of energy or brainpower.

Watch your television time. How often do you sit down to watch one show and end up watching several hours of television? Try turning the television on a half hour later than usual or turning it off a half hour earlier, and then take that time to do something else. Better yet, don't turn the television on unless there is a specific show you want to see and then turn it off when that show is over.

Do the worst task first. Get the least pleasurable task out of the way, and then the time in the rest of your day is free from worrying or thinking about it.

Use your lunch hour productively. If you have an hour for lunch, plan to spend 30 minutes eating and 30 minutes doing something that you want or need to do such as:

- Read a book.
- Take a nap.
- Take a walk.
- Pick up a few groceries.
- Make personal phone calls.
- Write a letter.
- Run a couple of quick errands.
- Just sit and think about whatever.

Fight back against procrastination. Think of procrastination as a crime that steals your time. Get tough on yourself. When you find yourself procrastinating, will yourself to stop what you're doing and begin what you need to be doing. If you do this consistently over a period of a few weeks, you will not only make better use of your time, but have more time left over each day as well.

ARE YOU GIVING YOURSELF ENOUGH TIME?

Many people (especially optimists!) have trouble managing their time because they underestimate how long activities really take. For example, if you are always late for work, try timing your drive tomorrow. You might find that it's a longer drive than you estimated and that you haven't been allowing yourself enough time to get there. While you're at it, time how long it takes from the moment you wake up to the moment you leave for work. Have you been underestimating there too? Having a more realistic estimate of the time it takes for routine tasks will keep you from running late and will help you be more productive throughout your day. So start timing now!

Let someone else do your grocery shopping. Grocery shopping services are popping up in cities all over the United States. You can order via telephone, fax, or on-line. You can't use coupons, but prices are fairly competitive and the service will deliver a minimum order for free at a time that's convenient for you.

Plan on leftovers. On the weekend or whenever you have more time, double or quadruple a recipe and freeze the leftovers for a quick, nutritious meal on a busier night. If you do this regularly, you'll spend a fraction of the time you spend now on cooking, which will free up more time to pursue other things.

Save yourself worry. Don't waste time trying to change things over which you have no control. Adapt your response if necessary, but accept the things you cannot change and move on.

Remind yourself every once in a while that all you really *must* do today is breathe in and breathe out. Nobody's going to die if you don't get everything on your list done today.

> **We always have time enough,**
> **if we will but use it aright.**
>
> — Johann Wolfgang von Goethe

Prioritize Now

Include on your "to do" list a realistic estimate of the time you will need to complete that activity or task. This will keep you from overcommitting.

Prioritize your day. What would you like to accomplish today? Which is the most important or difficult task on your list? Make that your first priority. Resist the temptation to do all the little things first "to get them out of the way." Continue prioritizing until you have a number next to each item on your list.

Assess your priorities. How do you determine your priorities? By asking yourself:

- What makes me happy?
- What is the one thing I most want to accomplish?
- What do I value most?

Create a buffer zone. When looking at how much time you have in a day and what you want to do, create a buffer zone around each activity that allows 10 to 25 percent more time than your estimate. This will accommodate unexpected delays, and you can spend unused buffer time any way you want to!

Consolidate. Plan ways to combine two or three similar tasks. For example, plan to write and send several e-mails when you log on to check received messages instead of logging on and off just to send one message. When you go upstairs or downstairs, take something with you that needs to be put away.

Cut your to-do list in half. Delegate anything that can be delegated and simply cross off those items that have been on your list forever. If these things were really important, you probably would have done them by now. Don't burden yourself with unnecessary tasks.

Keep your list to a minimum. On your daily to-do list, include only those tasks that you reasonably expect you can complete today.

Stay focused. Whether you're trying to unclutter a closet or write up a report at work, make a conscious choice to stick with it until the job is done. If it's an extensive project, decide before you begin how long you will work before taking a break or moving to another project. Limit distractions by turning off the telephone ringer or closing your door. The sooner you finish, the more time you'll have left over for you.

Know When to Quit

Pare down your commitments. Assess your involvement with various committees, boards, and clubs. Is the time you are spending on each of these commitments aligned with your values? Are you getting a sense of satisfaction or fulfillment from your involvement? Politely excuse yourself from those commitments that are creating any undue stress.

Ask for help. If you're doing more than your fair share of work around the house, ask other household members which tasks they would be willing to pick up. You might find that your husband doesn't mind vacuuming or that your teenager likes ironing.

Just say no. Don't let guilt make you take on more than you can handle. According to Miss Manners, the polite way to refuse is to offer an apology but no excuse. She suggests the following three polite denials:

- "Oh, I'm terribly sorry, but I can't."
- "I'd love to, but I'm afraid it's impossible."
- "Unfortunately, I can't, but I hope you can find someone."

At the end of the day, look back on your uncompleted tasks. Why were they left uncompleted? What held you up? How can you make sure they get done the next day?

Shuttle your shuttling responsibilities. A 1999 report by the Washington-based Surface Transportation Policy Project showed that American mothers with kids in school spend an average of 66 minutes each day driving. If it's safe, encourage children who are old enough to walk, bike, or skate to school and to after-school activities — or use public transportation. If other mothers you know are in the same time bind, see if you can work out a weekly schedule of pickups and drop-offs that provides all of you with a little extra free time.

Make Time for You

Designate a night to do your own thing. If your children are old enough to fend for themselves, consider making one night a week a night when they are all on their own. This can be your time to take a class, read, write, draw, or do whatever it is that brings you happiness. A night of alone time is also a good way to help children develop independence.

Set limits. Carve out a chunk of time that is your "do not disturb" time. Let everyone in your household know about this time and make it clear that you are to be interrupted only in case of emergency (give them your definition of "emergency," if necessary). Go through possible scenarios with them to make sure they understand. *Hint:* It's a lot easier on everyone if you spend your "do not disturb" time behind a closed door.

Get up earlier. If you can't find time for yourself during the day, try getting up before everyone else in your household. The wee hours of the morning are the most peaceful, quiet hours of the day — the ideal time to do something for yourself. Just be sure to go to bed a little earlier to ensure that you get enough sleep.

Strike one activity. Eliminate one activity that you do on a regular basis that provides you with little or no satisfaction and only adds to your sense of being overwhelmed.

Turn waiting time into free time. To make more productive use of time spent waiting for someone or something, keep a project box, basket, or bag near your telephone or in your car. Or simply use this time to relax and appreciate your surroundings.

Schedule in joyful activities. Plan time to do things that give you joy, such as spending time with your children, visiting friends and family, gardening, or whatever. Then schedule everything else around that time. Why should it be the reverse?

> *Time is the coin of your life.*
> *It is the only coin you have, and only you*
> *can determine how it will be spent.*
> *Be careful lest you let other people*
> *spend it for you.*
>
> — Carl Sandburg

Simplify Daily Living

In this chapter . . .

- *Seek Simplicity*
- *Celebrate Today*
- *Connect with Nature*
- *Stretch Your Mind*
- *Think Positively*
- *Nourish Your Soul*

I t's not easy to live simply in our complex world. But truly, life is as simple or as complicated as we make it. We can scurry here and there, trying to keep up with the quickening pace around us, or we can slow down and maybe even stop to enjoy the simpler pleasures — most of which can be found in our own homes and backyards.

Seek Simplicity

If you want to live a simpler life, the secret is to string together a series of simpler days, week after week, month after month, year after year. And that means making new choices about how you spend your time and energy — and learning to seek simplicity in all you do.

Shortcuts to a Simpler Life

Try to keep up with things. Keeping up is a lot easier than catching up.

Get into "wash and wear." Go through your clothes closets and drawers and pull out those articles of clothing that require special care, such as dry cleaning or ironing. Consider giving them away. When you buy new clothes, choose clothes that are machine washable and do not need to be ironed.

Get your hair styled in a way that is natural for it. If you have straight hair, get a good cut that accentuates the straightness. If you have curly hair, wear it curly. Try a new cut or styling product designed for your hair type. Going natural saves time and energy. If you've been thinking about getting a really short haircut, do it. Most short cuts look great with little or no blow-drying or fuss.

Put decisions in perspective. If you have trouble making a decision, ask yourself if it will matter in five years. If it won't, then you can relax in the knowledge that there is more than one "right" decision.

Do a little bit at a time. When you are faced with a task that you do not particularly relish, break it down into smaller tasks. Getting a small amount done in several spurts will make the chore much more pleasant.

Limit the number of choices you have to make on a daily basis. Pare down your wardrobe to your favorite outfits. Plan weekly meals in advance and post the plan on the refrigerator so you don't have to think about what's for dinner when you come home exhausted.

Ask kids to help. Give your children simple things to do that can help keep them (and you) organized. For example, keep a file rack on the kitchen counter or other common area and assign a different color folder to each child into which they are responsible for putting paperwork from school that requires your attention.

Resist the urge to do just one more thing or buy just one more thing.

Celebrate Today

We're always so busy thinking about and planning for the future. But what's the point when you waste the here and now? Don't focus on tomorrow; rejoice in what you have and make the most of *today.*

If It Feels Good, Do It

S-t-r-e-t-c-h. You don't even have to get out of bed to incorporate some stretching into your morning routine! Lie on your back and reach your arms up and over your head. With your toes pointing straight up to the ceiling, push out through your heels and reach your fingertips as far back as you can. Really stretch; hold for five seconds and release. Do it again, but this time stretch only through your right side. Then stretch only through your left side. Stretching gets the blood circulating to your head to give you a rush of energy to start your day.

Center yourself. Take a few moments each morning to think about how you will keep your life in balance today. If you know that you will need to work late, think about how you can squeeze some fun or relaxation into your day.

If you feel like dancing, go ahead and move your feet! If you feel like singing, belt out a tune at the top of your lungs!

Smile! Smiling can't solve all your problems, but the simple act of smiling makes you feel better automatically. Try it. Smile at everyone you pass today and see how it feels. Don't be surprised if people smile back, which will make you feel doubly good.

Explore the ordinary. While walking around your neighborhood, driving to work, or just sitting in your backyard, look more closely at the things around you. Look for something you've never noticed before. There is a simple but profound pleasure in discovery.

If you're feeling unappreciated, appreciate yourself.

Throw a party for no reason at all.

Yak, yak, yak. Social contact with friends may help keep your heart healthy. Think of face-to-face conversation as an alternative form of entertainment to television.

Gain a Fresh Perspective

Focus on what you have, rather than what you have not. Always, there will be people who have more wealth, charms, and abilities than you, just as there will always be people who have far less than you. Be content with what you have today.

Accept that you aren't perfect. It's okay — no one is perfect. People will still love you even when you make mistakes. They may even love you more for it. Accept that others have shortcomings too. Forgiving others' mistakes heals both parties, and frees us to learn from the past and move forward.

Make time for family and friends. Studies show that the happiest people are those who feel satisfied with their family life and friendships.

Don't double-book yourself. Sometimes, in our quest to make the most productive use of our time, we make one set of plans for early in the day and another set of plans for later in the day. But this doesn't allow for unexpected delays that might occur, and having to rush to the second activity takes away much of the enjoyment.

Tomorrow is another day. If grief or sorrow, pain or suffering does not allow you to rejoice today, remember that this too shall pass. Every once in a while on our journey, we have to go through a dark tunnel. Challenge yourself to keep moving and eventually you will see the light on the other side.

Stick to the truth. Do your best to speak the truth about all things. If you have a tendency to tell little white lies (or big, brazen lies), then you have to remember everything you tell everyone. This not only creates stress, but also eats up a lot of energy. Being true to yourself and honest with others will set you free.

> *Finish every day and be done with it.*
> *You have done what you could.*
>
> — Ralph Waldo Emerson

Cultivate close friendships. It is better to have one or two really close friends than a dozen acquaintances. Good friends are those with whom you can talk about nothing and anything. They let you be yourself — and love you anyway. They bring joy and happiness to your life if you let them. Robert Louis Stevenson once wrote, "A friend is a present you give yourself."

Connect with Nature

There's a whole other world out there that is moving at the same pace today as it did thousands of years ago. The sun rises each morning with precision and certainty and sets each evening as it has since the beginning of time. When was the last time you watched the sun set or rise, or took a walk around the block to enjoy the sights and sounds of nature?

Appreciate the Everyday "Wonders"

Tune in to the sounds of nature. There's something reassuring and soothing about nature's rhythms and sounds. The sounds of nature actually help ease stress, and may help keep at bay those physical problems with strong links to your emotions, such as heart attack and high blood pressure.

Bring nature inside. If you can't get "back to nature" as often as you'd like, try listening to audiotapes of nature sounds. Get comfortable, close your eyes, and listen to the sounds of woodland birds and crickets or the steady rhythm of ocean waves breaking over rocks.

Do nothing. Schedule some time for doing nothing at all except to sit and daydream and wonder at the universe. You can do it anywhere, but if you walk to a peaceful place in nature, so much the better.

Explore your neighborhood. Go outside and look for things you hadn't noticed before — even in your own backyard. Just take notice of what you see and any thoughts or ideas that pop into your head. Taking a closer look not only encourages curiosity, but also can lead to making some amazing connections. And it's fun!

Sit outside at dusk and watch it get dark.

Take nourishment from the sun. Sunlight helps your skin make vitamin D, which, in turn, helps your body absorb calcium and then deposit it in your bones and teeth. Just 10 to 15 minutes of direct sun exposure to your face, arms, and hands three times a week stimulates all the vitamin D your body needs. For more prolonged exposure to sun, be sure to apply sunscreen.

Join a bicycling or hiking club and participate in regular outings.

TRY NATURE JOURNALING

Nature journaling, quite simply, is the act of recording your observations about the natural world at a particular time and place and becoming, in the process, directly involved in that world. Try the following exercise, excerpted from *Nature Journaling: Learning to Observe and Connect with the World Around You* by Clare Walker Leslie and Charles E. Roth (Storey Books, 1998):

> Go find a piece of paper; it doesn't matter what type or size. Find any pencil, marker, or drawing tool. Now gather up your eyes, take a deep breath, and ask yourself: "What is happening outdoors, this particular season, this time of day, and in this particular place where I live?" (You can be outdoors, or inside looking out.) Draw a cloud, a bird flying by, a tree branch, ivy vines on a building wall, a potted plant, or a garden flower. Don't judge your drawing. You are not an artist yet. You are a scientist, simply recording what you see, in this moment in time. Be very quiet, be very still. Slow your breathing and think only "bud," "plant," "bird." After one minute or less, no more, write what you drew and go on to the next sighting, keeping it relevant to season, time of day, and place.

Stretch Your Mind

Learning contributes to our sense of general well-being, perhaps because it helps us better understand ourselves and our world. When you make it a lifelong pursuit, learning can help simplify your life by opening your eyes to possibilities you never knew existed.

Expand Your Horizons

Read. It's amazing what you can learn by reading — even when you're not actively trying to learn!

Try new things. Push your limits — physically, socially, emotionally, intellectually, and spiritually — and allow yourself the opportunity to discover and appreciate the greatness within you.

Spend free time really getting to know your area. Read up on the history of your village, town, or city. Visit its gardens, parks, recreational areas, and natural resources. What does each one have to offer and what is the best time of year to go there?

Better yourself through learning. Whether you want to advance your career, change careers, or simply better your mind, take deliberate action to continue your education. Set learning goals by following your curiosity.

Expand your universe. Just as a goldfish grows larger in a larger bowl, people grow according to the size of their world — not physically, but mentally. Actively incorporate learning into your daily life by reading, listening, experimenting, observing, and thinking. Just beware: Expanding your mind may transform your life! Here are a few suggestions for expanding your universe:

- Get a library card — and use it.
- Visit museums and historical landmarks.
- Listen to books on tape while doing your housework.
- Attend workshops and seminars.
- Learn how to do something you've always wanted to do.
- Join a book discussion group.
- Try a food you've never tried before.
- Drive a different way home from work.
- See what happens when you do "this" instead of "that."

Share thoughts and ideas. Plan and participate in activities that enable you to meet and spend time with other people who share your values.

Learn on-line. If you have access to the Internet, you have volumes upon volumes of knowledge at your fingertips. Start exploring and see where your explorations lead you. You can even take some college classes on-line.

Get college credit for your life experience. Most colleges recognize the educational value of your experiences, which provides an opportunity for you to get a jump-start on a college degree. You may be able to create a portfolio to document your experiential learning — and earn up to 36 college credits. You also may take what might be considered the final exam in any number of subjects and gain credit that way. Ask at your local college about College-Level Examination Program (CLEP) tests, the Advanced Placement Program (APP), and the American College Testing Program (ACT-PEP).

Think Positively

When you think positively, it's positively contagious. Change your attitude about one aspect of your life and watch how it automatically improves other areas of your life as well.

It's What You Make of It

Keep your eyes open for all things good. When you look for the best in people, places, and things, that's what you will find.

Think good thoughts. What you choose to think and believe and say right now will shape your future. Upon awakening, while working, and before going to bed, notice what you are thinking. Is it positive or negative?

EXPECTATION OR PREDICTION?

There's a wonderful story in *The Way of the Peaceful Warrior* by Dan Millman that illustrates how our attitudes shape our experiences. It goes something like this:

A wise old man is resting at the side of the road. A traveler approaches and asks him if he knows what the people are like in the town up ahead. The wise old man asks him, "What were the people like in the town you just came from?" to which the traveler replies, "Oh, they were rude and nasty and I couldn't trust anyone." And so the wise old man tells him that the people in the town up ahead are exactly the same. And the traveler trudges off. A little while later, another traveler stops to ask the wise old man if he knows what the people are like up in the town ahead. The wise man responds with the same question he posed to the first traveler, to which the second traveler replies, "Oh, they are the most wonderful and loving and caring people a man could ever hope to know." And so the wise old man tells the traveler that the people in the town up ahead are all that and more.

Find the silver lining. For every action, there is an equal and opposite reaction. Look for the positive in everything negative that happens in your life.

Attitude is everything. Two little boys were playing on the beach at the edge of the ocean when suddenly a large wave rushed over them. When the wave receded, one boy was crying and the other was laughing. They were both hit by the same wave, but each perceived it very differently. Remember that it's not *what* happens to us, but what *attitude* we choose that shapes our experiences.

Keep a "can do" attitude. It will help you make friends and achieve whatever your heart desires.

Accept serendipity. *Webster's* defines *serendipity* as "the finding of valuable or agreeable things not sought for." As you think about what would bring more meaning and satisfaction to your life, pay close attention to what is going on around you. Serendipitous events happen all the time; we just don't always recognize them!

Turn negative energy into positive energy. By taking charge of your thoughts, you can turn them into a powerful source of inner strength and confidence. Let's say, for example, that your best friend becomes upset with you about something you've done. Your initial response is hurt or anger (negative energy) because you think you've done nothing wrong. But then you think about what happened and, in reviewing the situation, you discover something about yourself that you decide to change. In this way, you can be thankful for the experience.

Acknowledge negative thoughts. In her book *Heart Thoughts,* Louise L. Hay says, "You don't have to fight your thoughts when you want to change things. When that negative voice comes up, you can say: 'Thank you for sharing.' You are not giving your power over to the negative thought, and yet you are not denying that it is there. You are saying: 'Okay, you're there and thank you for sharing, and I'm choosing to do something else. I don't want to buy into that anymore, I want to create another way of thinking.' Don't fight your thoughts. Acknowledge them and go beyond them."

Walk tall. Good posture makes you look better and feel better. So stand up straight, lift your chin so that it's parallel to the floor, tuck in your abdomen and buttocks, and relax your shoulders.

Do You Feel Lucky?

Marc Myers, author of *How to Make Luck: Seven Secrets Lucky People Use to Succeed,* believes that if you can change your behavior, you can improve your luck. He says that luck is different from chance. You can't control or predict chance, but you can control your response to what happens to you. He also believes that projecting an image of being lucky attracts luck your way. Here are a few of Myers's suggestions to give yourself a fortunate image and boost your luck:

- Believe that you are lucky and you will act luckier.

- If something bad happens, get over it as quickly as you can.
- Be humble about your good fortune.
- Project confidence without being cocky.
- Think before you act, and if you make a mistake, admit it.
- Be generous without expecting anything in return.

Nourish Your Soul

One way to simplify daily living is to open your heart to your community and to your Higher Power. Find meaningful ways to connect with friends and strangers alike. Establishing a link with yourself and others is like feeding your soul.

Take Action

Be of service. Whether you volunteer for community service projects, help at a school, or visit senior citizens, by giving of your time you help make the world a better place and bring more fulfillment to your own life.

Cultivate close friendships. Spend time with people who support your efforts to live according to your values. Attend services with a community of believers. Look for and attend a Voluntary Simplicity group in your area. Or start your own support group or study circle among friends, neighbors, or coworkers.

Practice random acts of kindness. A good deed or an altruistic act can do wonders for your heart — physically, emotionally, and spiritually. Try these random acts of kindness:

- Brush snow off a stranger's car in a parking lot.
- Send flowers anonymously to someone you know who could use a little cheering up.
- Leave candies on the chairs of coworkers while they are at lunch.
- If someone is waiting to pull out into traffic and it is safe to do, allow that person to go ahead of you.
- Pay the toll for the car behind you at a tollbooth.
- Leave store coupons near the coupon items on supermarket shelves.
- Place a quarter in a gumball machine or coin return of a pay phone.
- Send an anonymous contribution to a favorite charity.

Withhold criticism or judgment. The more you refrain from passing judgment on others, the less you will hear yourself.

Converse with your Higher Power — aloud or in your head. Ask for help during difficult times. Pray for the welfare of a friend or family member. Offer thanks for the beauty and goodness in the world. Verbalize your thoughts and dilemmas.

Give yourself a 15-minute time-out every day. Spend it quietly doing nothing or doing something that brings you joy.

Appreciate your surroundings. Look for beauty in the people, places, and things that you come into contact with each day.

Give a hug, or ask for one.

Make Sunday (or one day a week) a day of rest. Plan to share time with family and friends. Drive up north to your Aunt Martha's. Invite your neighbors for a cookout. Don't feel that you have to do anything special; just be together.

Keep a good-news journal. Take a few minutes at the end of each day to write down the good things that happened throughout your day. On a day when you're feeling down, read through your journal.

Choose to be happy.

Resources

Health & Wellness

Fitness Link
www.fitnesslink.com
This informative on-line resource provides practical, in-depth information about nutrition, exercise, lifestyle changes, mind/body, and fitness programs, with tips for getting started. It also includes the latest fitness news, updated daily.

Health Central
www.healthcentral.com
Established by Dr. Dean Edell, this site is a reliable source of information about a variety of health conditions, indexed A–Z. Click on "Free Personal Health Profile" for a personal health risk assessment. You also can sign up to receive a free weekly e-mail newsletter with news and information personally tailored to your interests.

Mayo Clinic On-Line
www.mayohealth.com
The Mayo Clinic site includes a searchable library, practical advice for first aid, health centers for news and information about treating specific diseases and conditions, quizzes and health assessments, and even a virtual cookbook with a variety of tasty, healthful recipes. Sign up for a free e-mail bulletin with weekly updates.

Money & Finances

Bankrate.com
www.bankrate.com
Bankrate.com provides objective financial data and research and editorial information to help consumers make informed decisions about mortgages, credit cards, new and used auto loans, money market accounts and CDs, checking and ATM fees, home equity lines and loans, and online banking fees.

Consumer Credit Counseling Service
(800) 388-2227 (national office)
A nonprofit community organization, CCCS provides free, confidential financial counseling on budgeting and credit management. Its debt repayment plan is a legal alternative to bankruptcy that allows financially stressed consumers to repay creditors over time. Check the Yellow Pages of your local telephone directory or call toll-free information to find an office near you.

Dollar Stretcher Club
The Dollar Stretcher
P.O. Box 23785
Fort Lauderdale, FL 33307
(954) 772-1696
www.stretcher.com
The Dollar Stretcher offers a virtual meeting place for people who are helping each other to gain control of their finances through frugal living. For a schedule of meetings, go to www.stretcher.com

and click on "Dollar Stretcher Club." You can also get current and past issues of a weekly newsletter called *Living Better . . . For Less.* Or send $2 to the address above for a sample issue.

Simple Living

Balancing Act
P.O. Box 309
Ghent, NY 12075-0309
members.aol.com/balancinga/ba.html
Balancing Act is a bimonthly newsletter that helps people save money and simplify their lives. For a sample issue, send $1 plus a SASE to the above address or visit the Web page. To subscribe for a year, send $6 along with your name and address.

Life On Purpose Institute
P.O. Box 834
Flat Rock, NC 28731-0834
(800) 668-0183
(828) 697-9239
www.lifeonpurpose.com
The Life On Purpose Institute is dedicated to purposeful service, mindful and abundant simplicity, and spiritual serenity. Its Web site features inspiring stories about people who are living purposeful lives. The site offers a self-test to help you determine if you are living life on purpose. It also offers a free subscription to *Purposeful Pondering* e-zine and a free five-part virtual seminar that will arrive in your e-mail over a week's time.

The Simple Living Network
P.O. Box 233
Trout Lake, WA 98650
(800) 318-5725
www.simpleliving.net
The Simple Living Network is an on-line service with thousands of pages of information, tools, and resources for people who want to live a simpler, healthier, more environmentally conscious lifestyle. The Web site features a free weekly e-zine.

Simple Times
simple-times-subscribe@egroups.com
A free e-mail newsletter for simple, frugal living from the author of *Frozen Assets: How to Cook for a Day and Eat for a Month.* Regular topics include frugality, using leftovers, freezer meals, shopping tips, food prep and storage, and more. To subscribe to this biweekly e-mail newsletter, send a blank e-mail message to the above address.

Happiness comes from the capacity to feel deeply, to enjoy simply, to think freely, to be needed.

— Storm Jameson

Index

Other Storey Books
You Will Enjoy

Feng Shui Tips for a Better Life, by David Daniel Kennedy. With this easy-to-use and easy-to-understand resource, even beginners can use the ancient Chinese art of feng shui to attract health, romance, career opportunities, and more! Paperback. 176 pages. ISBN 1-58017-038-2.

50 Simple Ways to Pamper Yourself, by Stephanie Tourles. With these easy, inspiring ideas and simple recipes you'll learn how to integrate much-needed moments of nourishment, relaxation, and rejuvenation into your everyday life. Paperback. 144 pages. ISBN 1-58017-210-5.

Keeping Life Simple, by Karen Levine. This valuable book helps readers assess what's really satisfying and then offers hundreds of tips for creating a lifestyle that is more rewarding. Paperback. 160 pages. ISBN 0-88266-943-5.

Keeping Fitness Simple, by Porter Shimer. Shimer's book offers fun, easy fitness tips that don't involve expensive health clubs or exhausting workouts. Paperback. 176 pages. ISBN 1-58017-034-X.

Keeping Work Simple, by Don Aslett and Carol Cartaino. Well-known time management expert and crusader against clutter Don Aslett recommends practical ideas for simplifying any work environment to achieve maximum performance. Paperback. 160 pages. ISBN 0-88266-996-6.

Unclutter Your Home, by Donna Smallin. This book offers hundreds of concrete tips for sorting, evaluating, and getting rid of all those material items that get in the way of a simplified lifestyle. Learn how to store items efficiently, avoid old habits, and create a more pleasant and uplifting environment. Paperback. 192 pages. ISBN 1-58017-108-7.

These and other Storey books are available at your bookstore, farm store, garden center, or directly from Storey Books, Schoolhouse Road, Pownal, Vermont 05261, or by calling 1-800-441-5700. Or visit our website at www.storeybooks.com.